Thomson Round Hall Nutcases:

Evidence

UNITED KINGDOM

Sweet & Maxwell Ltd
London

AUSTRALIA

Law Book Co. Ltd
Sydney

CANADA AND THE USA

Carswell
Toronto

NEW ZEALAND

Brookers
Wellington

SINGAPORE AND MALAYSIA

Sweet and Maxwell
Singapore and Kuala Lumpur

Thomson Round Hall

Evidence

Neil van Dokkum

DUBLIN
THOMSON ROUND HALL
2007

Published in 2007 by
Thomson Round Hall
43 Fitzwilliam Place
Dublin 2
Ireland

Typeset by
Thomson Round Hall

Printed by
ColourBooks, Dublin

978-1-85800-463-1

A catalogue record for this book
is available from the British Library.

For Dad and Leon.

Acknowledgments

This book was written as a companion to the *Nutshell* on Evidence, and my sincere thanks to Ross Gorman for allowing me access to his excellent work whilst it was still in draft form. My thanks also to the highly professional people at Thomson Round Hall, in particular, Susan Rossney for her support and gentle reminders, and Frieda Donohue, who did all the hard work at the end.

To my office colleagues at WIT—Walter O'Leary, Grainne Callanan, Elliott Payne, and Albert Keating—thanks again for your support; and to my fellow Evidence lecturer, Cyril Crawley, many thanks for your expertise in introducing me to the Irish law of evidence.

To my lovely Fiona, who has spent days proofreading my efforts, and correcting my dodgy grammar, my eternal thanks; and to my whole family for having to do without me when I disappeared to work on the next chapter, my gratitude.

Preface

The subject of evidence often gets bad press for a number of misguided reasons, amongst them that "it gets the bad guys off through technicalities", "it is too complicated", "it is illogical", etc.

None of these are true—the law of evidence doesn't just help the "bad guys", but the "good guys" as well; offenders escape punishment because those that are meant to be enforcing the law do not do their jobs properly, it has nothing to do with "legal technicalities". The rules of evidence are largely consistent and simple enough when you become familiar with them. If obeyed, they will reward.

As this case-book will hopefully show, the judgments handed down by our courts are a very important slice of social history—there are some fascinating stories within and behind these cases, encouraging the student to read and find out more.

I hope this book will introduce students to the subject in a positive and helpful fashion.

Neil van Dokkum
February, 2007

Table of Contents

Table of Cases

ENGLISH CASES

PRIVY COUNCIL CASES

AUSTRALIAN CASES

Evidence

CANADIAN CASES

US CASES

ECHR CASES

Table of Legislation

CONSTITUTION OF IRELAND

IRISH STATUTES

ENGLISH STATUTES

CANADIAN STATUTES

EUROPEAN LEGISLATION

STATUTORY INSTRUMENTS

1. An Introduction to the Law of Evidence

WHAT IS EVIDENCE?

Evidence is information placed before a hearing. The hearing could be a trial in court, an enquiry before a judge or some other presiding officer, or even a disciplinary hearing at an employer's premises. This information consists of facts and inferences (conclusions drawn from the facts) and is designed to prove or disprove issues that are in dispute and about which the hearing must decide. The aim of any litigation lawyer is to present evidence in such a way that it will favourably influence the decision of the judge (or other presiding officer) on the matter in dispute.

Evidence is made up of various types of factual information. It can be testimony, documentary or real. Testimony is evidence given by a witness. Documentary evidence is the evidence of contents of documents (for example, a bus timetable or a letter) but also refers to anything in which information of any description is recorded, and may therefore include such items as films and video recordings. Paradoxically, although affidavits (sworn statements) are essentially documents, they are categorised as testimonial evidence. Finally, real evidence is evidence made up of things that must be perceived through the five senses—seen, heard, smelled, touched or tasted— in order to fully appreciate the significance of that evidence.

These are the traditional groups of evidence found in judicial proceedings, and are collectively called judicial evidence. In the modern courtroom we have concepts like electronic or computer evidence, and genetic or DNA evidence, which do not always fit comfortably into these traditional categories, whilst other types of evidence, like hearsay and circumstantial evidence, and the practice of judicial notice, have established an independent identity of their own. Despite these developments, all evidence can be fitted into one of the three traditional groups of judicial evidence.

Our law of evidence is really an assorted collection of rules of exclusion, rather than inclusion. The rules of evidence have been developed not to assist a party in bringing evidence to court and so win the case, but rather to prevent or prohibit that party from using some or all of this evidence because it may be regarded as unreliable, or untested, or because the potential prejudice caused by its admission outweighs its usefulness (sometimes described as the probative value of evidence).

THE ADMISSIBILITY OF EVIDENCE

Key principle: The starting point of the law of evidence is that evidence is admissible if relevant (material) and reliable (credible). Even where these requirements are satisfied, the court might decide not to admit evidence because of reasons of policy—for example, where the evidence was obtained as a result of an illegal or unethical act.

Attorney-General v O'Brien [1965]

Gerald O'Brien was convicted of housebreaking and stealing and Patrick O'Brien was convicted of housebreaking and receiving stolen property.

The stolen property was found during a search by members of the Garda Síochána of a house at No.118, Captain's Road, where the O'Briens lived. The search warrant, by some mistake, described the premises not as "118 Captain's Road, Crumlin", but as "118 Cashel Road, Crumlin".

There was no question of deliberate alteration of the warrant and it was not clear whether the Garda sergeant noticed the mistake before searching the premises, but the search had been conducted without a valid warrant. The O'Briens sought to have the evidence of the stolen property excluded.

Held: The illegal search was the result of an oversight rather than a deliberate and conscious violation of constitutional rights, and the evidence should be admitted. *The People (at the suit of the Attorney-General) v Gerald O'Brien and Patrick O'Brien (1)* [1965] I.R. 142.

Key Principle: All evidence must be relevant to the issues before the court, which are, in turn, determined by the facts in issue, which are the facts in dispute between the parties that must be proved in order to succeed in a claim before the court.

DPP v Shortt (No.1) [2002]

Frank Shortt had successfully applied to have his conviction quashed on the grounds that new and relevant facts had surfaced before and during his trial, and these were concealed from him, thereby compromising his defence.

Shortt thereafter applied to the court for a certificate of miscarriage of justice, which would have entitled him to compensation. He led evidence in support of the claim and the DPP led evidence in rebuttal. The cases of both parties were then closed.

Thereafter, the DPP sought leave to re-open its case and lead the evidence of Colm Quinn, who would testify that Shortt knew there were people selling illegal drugs in his pub.

Held: The present application was concerned with the question of whether there had been a miscarriage of justice against Shortt which entitled him to compensation. The issue before the court was not whether Shortt was guilty or not guilty, as that could only be decided after a proper criminal trial.

The granting of a certificate would not necessarily mean that Shortt was innocent, and therefore a positive finding of innocence was not necessary for the granting of a certificate. Accordingly, the evidence of Quinn was irrelevant to the issues before the court. *In the matter of an application pursuant to s.9 of the Criminal Procedure Act, 1993: The People (at the suit of the Director of Public Prosecutions) v Frank Shortt (No.1)* [2002] 2 I.R. 686.

Key Principle: Evidence is admissible when it can be properly received by a court as a matter of law. As the question of the admissibility of evidence is a matter of law, as opposed to fact, it is decided by the trial judge, and not by the jury.

The weight of the evidence is the probative force of that evidence. In other words, it is a measure of the contribution the evidence can make to resolving the facts at issue or to proving the fact or facts that it was adduced to prove. This is a question of fact (as opposed to a question of law), and will be decided by the jury in a jury trial.

DPP v Lynch [1982]

Christopher Lynch entered a house that a landlord had asked him to paint. He discovered the dead body of a woman who had lived in the house. Lynch contacted the Gardaí and, at 4.00 p.m., he went to a station to make a statement, which he completed at 7.45 p.m. In the statement he described how he had found the deceased and confirmed that he had been in the house on the previous day, a Saturday.

Lynch remained in the Garda station for the whole of the Sunday night and he was questioned almost continually until 8.30 a.m. on the next day, Monday. At 10.00 a.m. on that day he was brought to another Garda station where he was interrogated until 2.00 p.m., when he confessed to the murder of the woman. Having slept for a few hours, he was awakened at 6.00 p.m. on the Monday. He completed a written statement confessing that he had killed the woman at some time before 2.30 p.m. on the Saturday. These statements were the only evidence against him.

Held: The treatment of Lynch whilst he was in custody had been so oppressive that his confession could not be regarded as voluntary. The confession was excluded from the evidence. *The People (at the suit of the Director of Public Prosecutions) v Christopher Anthony Lynch* [1982] I.R. 64.

THE BURDEN OF PROOF

The party before the court that needs to prove the facts at issue is said to bear the burden of proof. As a general rule, the plaintiff in a civil trial, and the prosecution in a criminal trial, bears the burden of proof to prove the facts at issue and so succeed in their claim or prosecution respectively.

The legal burden of proof, sometimes known as the "probative burden", the "persuasive burden", "the risk of non-persuasion", or "the onus", remains fixed throughout the trial, and is placed upon the party who must ultimately prove the facts at issue and, in so doing, satisfy the court that it is entitled to succeed in its claim.

The evidential burden, sometimes known as a "provisional burden" or "tactical burden", on the other hand, moves from one party to the other throughout the trial. The evidential burden is placed on a party as a duty to lead evidence in order to initially create a *prima facie* case (a case that requires a reply), or rebut a *prima facie* point or inference made by their opponent.

Key Principle: The fact that a party bearing an evidential burden fails to rebut that burden does not necessarily mean that the party will lose the trial, as the party bearing the legal burden still carries the overall burden of succeeding in its claim or prosecution.

O'Leary v Attorney-General [1995]

Donal O'Leary was convicted of being a member of an unlawful organisation, namely the IRA. Section 3(2) of the Offences Against the State (Amendment) Act of 1972 provides that where a Garda officer not below the rank of chief superintendent gives evidence that he believes the defendant was a member of an unlawful organisation, the statement shall be evidence that the defendant was a member of an unlawful organisation. Section 24 of the same Act says that where the defendant is found in possession of an incriminating document issued by an unlawful organisation, this shall be evidence that the defendant was a member of that unlawful organisation.

At his trial, evidence was led that O'Leary was in possession of IRA posters at the time of his arrest, and in addition a chief superintendent gave evidence that he believed that O'Leary was a member of the IRA.

O'Leary argued that these provisions were unconstitutional as they shifted the burden of proof onto him, which offended the presumption of innocence.

Held: When using the phrase "burden of proof" in this context, what was meant was that O'Leary assumed an evidential burden of rebutting a *prima facie* case (on a balance of probabilities) that he was a member of an illegal organisation. His failure to rebut the *prima facie* case did not automatically mean conviction, as the State would still need to prove his guilt beyond a reasonable doubt. The appeal was refused. *Donal O'Leary v Attorney-General* [1995] 2 I.L.R.M. 259.

Woolmington v DPP [1935]

Reginald Woolmington's wife left him and returned to her mother. Woolmington bought a shotgun, and shortened the gun with a hacksaw so that it would fit into his jacket pocket. He dropped the severed pieces and the hacksaw into a nearby stream. He visited his wife at her mother's house. His evidence was that he wanted to frighten her into coming back to him by threatening to shoot himself if she did not. According to his version of events, when he took out the shotgun, it went off and hit his wife. In other words, he admitted to shooting her but claimed that the shooting was accidental. He was charged with murder.

Evidence was led that Woolmington had written a letter which contained the following: "Her mother is no good on this earth but have no more cartridges only 2 one for her and one for me. I am of a sound mind now. Forgive me for all trouble caused. Good bye ALL. I love Violet with all my heart. Reg."

Woolmington testified that he had written the letter after killing his wife as he intended to kill himself thereafter, but his father had persuaded him not to kill himself, and he had turned himself in.

The trial judge instructed the jury that once it was proved that Woolmington had killed his wife, the jury was obliged to presume that he had murdered her unless he could prove that he was not guilty of murder. This finding was confirmed by the Court of Appeal and Woolmington appealed to the House of Lords.

Held: The House of Lords upheld Woolmington's appeal on the basis that the proof of the killing gave rise only to a provisional inference of his guilt. In other words, an evidential burden was placed on Woolmington to show that the shooting was accidental, but his failure to do this did not automatically mean that he had to be found guilty. The legal burden of proof remained on the prosecution throughout, and it was open to the jury to find that the prosecution had not proven guilt beyond a reasonable doubt—in other words, the prosecution needed to show beyond a reasonable doubt that Woolmington intentionally killed his wife, knowing that he was doing wrong when he fired the gun. The appeal was allowed and the conviction quashed. *Reginald Woolmington v Director of Public Prosecutions* [1935] A.C. 462.

Brown v Rolls Royce Ltd [1960]

John Brown was employed by Rolls Royce as a machine oiler from 1952 to 1955. His hands were constantly in contact with oil. In 1954 he contracted dermatitis as a result of this contact. Rolls Royce did not supply barrier cream, as there was a view that it did not prevent dermatitis, although there were strong differences in medical opinion. Rolls Royce relied on its medical officer for advice on the precautions to be taken against dermatitis, and, on his advice, barrier cream was not one of the precautions required in their system.

Evidence was led that *Rozalex No.1* barrier cream was commonly supplied by employers to men doing work of this kind, but there was no evidence as to what, if any, other precautions they took. In addition, it was not proved that barrier cream was an effective precaution against dermatitis for men engaged in similar work to Brown, nor that it would probably have prevented him from contracting dermatitis.

Held: The evidence of Brown about precautions taken by other employers created an evidential burden on Rolls Royce to explain why the cream was not supplied to Brown, or alternatively to show that it was supplied to Brown but never used by him.

The onus was on Brown to show that Rolls Royce had been negligent and that its negligence had caused the injury. It was not right to create an artificial division of the onus of proof by taking some of the findings of fact separately so as to suggest that they raised a presumption of negligence which Rolls Royce must rebut.

Lord Denning held that the legal burden of proof, properly so called, which is imposed by the law itself, must be distinguished from the provisional burden which is raised by the state of the evidence. *John Brown v Rolls Royce Ltd* [1960] 1 All E.R. 577.

Res ipsa loquitur

In the civil law the legal burden will usually rest on the plaintiff to prove the necessary facts in order to secure judgment. An important exception to this general rule is the doctrine of *res ipsa loquitur*, which means "let the acts speak for themselves" and means that if an accident is caused by something under the control of the defendant, in circumstances where an accident would not usually occur unless there was negligence, then negligence is presumed on the part of the defendant.

Key Principle: The doctrine of *res ipsa loquitur* raises a presumption of negligence that can be rebutted by showing that reasonable care was practised by the defendant.

Lindsay v Mid-Western Health Board [1993]

During the month of March 1982, Beatrice Lindsay, an infant at the time, was admitted to a hospital under the control of the Mid-Western Health Board (MWHB). An emergency appendectomy was carried out under general anaesthetic. After the operation it appeared initially that Beatrice was beginning to regain consciousness, but she experienced a series of seizures, and went into a coma. Beatrice was subsequently diagnosed as suffering from irreversible brain damage. She never regained consciousness and, at the time of the High Court hearing, had been in a deep coma for 18 years.

Beatrice sued the MWHB for damages for negligence and argued that her condition was as a result of a reduction in, or withdrawal of, her oxygen supply. Secondly, Beatrice pleaded *res ipsa loquitur*, submitting that there was an onus upon the medical practitioners to explain her condition. She argued that she was healthy when she entered the hospital for what is considered a routine operation, involving no special risks, and she had been entirely in the care and control of the MWHB. The onus was consequently cast upon the MWHB to explain her injury and to show that it had not resulted from any negligence on its part.

The MWHB denied that Beatrice's condition was the result of a lack of oxygen, and argued that her condition was the result of a viral infection in respect of which it was not liable.

Held: The doctrine of *res ipsa loquitur* applied on the facts. However, it was still open to the MWHB to rebut this doctrine by showing that all reasonable care was exercised. *Beatrice Lindsay (an infant suing by her aunt and next friend Nora Phelan) v Mid-Western Health Board* [1993] 2 I.R. 147.

Commentary

This is a somewhat controversial rule and part of the controversy concerns the question of whether the doctrine shifts the legal burden or the evidential burden. The court in *Lindsay* seemed to prefer the view that the doctrine only shifts the evidential burden, with the overall burden of proving negligence remaining with the plaintiff.

Many jurisdictions have rejected the doctrine in its entirety, arguing that the same solution can be obtained through more traditional means.

THE CIVIL STANDARD VERSUS THE CRIMINAL STANDARD OF PROOF

The standard of proof required in civil cases is known as the "balance of probabilities".

The civil standard involves a comparative, rather than a quantitative, test. The plaintiff needs to show that its case, or version of events, is inherently probable, and is also more probable than the defendant's version.

On the other hand, the criminal standard is "proof beyond reasonable doubt". Although higher than the civil standard of proof, the criminal standard of proof does not mean proof beyond all doubt or proof beyond the slightest doubt, as this would mean that all offenders would walk free. A reasonable doubt exists where the probabilities of the accused being not guilty can be regarded as reasonable on the grounds of generally accepted human knowledge and experience. Where it can be said by a reasonable person that the version of the accused may be true, the prosecution has not proven its case beyond a reasonable doubt. This is not the same as saying that the court or jury must believe the version of the accused, as it is enough that it may be true.

Key Principle: As a general rule, the standard of proof "beyond a reasonable doubt" is used only in the criminal law.

Miller v Minister of Pensions [1947]

Captain Miller served in the army from 1915 until his death in 1944, when he died of cancer of the gullet. Mrs Miller, his widow, claimed for the higher pension granted to widows of soldiers whose death was "due to war service". A tribunal rejected her claim on the basis that Captain Miller's death was not due to war service. She appealed that decision.

Held: That where a serviceman falls ill during his service which leads to his death or discharge, there is a compelling presumption that it was due to war service unless the evidence proves beyond reasonable doubt that the disease was not attributable or aggravated by war service. On the other hand, where the man was fit on his discharge, and later falls ill, there is no compelling presumption in his favour, and the matter must be decided on a balance of probabilities.

In this matter an officer serving in the Western Desert reported sick and was found to be suffering from cancer of the gullet. He died within a month. The aetiology of cancer is unknown. There was evidence that for all practical purposes cancer is not looked on as contagious or infectious, and that cancer of the gullet is unrelated to employment and environment. The tribunal dismissed the widow's claim to a pension on the ground that the probabilities were that war service played no part. The tribunal could reasonably come to that conclusion, and, therefore, the widow's appeal had to be dismissed. *Miller v Minister of Pensions* [1947] 2 All E.R. 372.

PRESUMPTIONS

A presumption says that something is so until the contrary is proved. A presumption of fact is no more than an inference of common sense, based upon what usually happens or is assumed to usually happen. So, when a new ship is launched, there is a presumption of seaworthiness, as it is presumed that nobody would be foolish enough to launch a new ship that was not seaworthy. A presumption of fact can be rebutted by leading evidence to the contrary.

An irrebuttable presumption of law is just an ordinary rule of substantive law that is dressed up to look like a rule of evidence. For example, the irrebuttable presumption that a young child is incapable of having a guilty mind (*mens rea*) could simply be written as the rule that "no person under the age of 12 years shall be charged with, or convicted of, a criminal offence".

Key Principle: An irrebuttable presumption of law binds a court to accept the fact that it presumes.

Maher v Attorney-General [1973]

John Maher was convicted of driving under the influence of alcohol in terms of the Road Traffic Act of 1961. This Act said that a certificate stating that a specimen of a person's blood contained a specified concentration of alcohol should be "conclusive evidence" that, when the specimen was taken, the concentration of alcohol in that person's blood was as specified in the certificate. Maher was convicted on the basis of such a certificate. He appealed his conviction and argued that, in effect, this certificate created an irrebuttable presumption of law and was therefore unconstitutional as it negated the presumption of innocence.

Held: The Supreme Court agreed with Maher as the word "conclusive" had the effect of infringing upon the judicial power of the District Justice at Maher's trial: the decision of innocence or guilt was effectively taken out of the judge's hands by the certificate. *John P. Maher v the Attorney-General and Francis T. Murphy* [1973] I.R. 140.

Key Principle: A rebuttable presumption of law compels a provisional acceptance of a fact, until that fact is disproved by evidence. Where a statute creates a rebuttable presumption of law which is to be exercised by a criminal court, the accused need only rebut that presumption on a balance of probabilities, and not beyond a reasonable doubt.

DPP v Best [2000]

Christine Best was charged under the School Attendance Act of 1926 for failing to send her children to school. It is a defence under this Act to show that the child is receiving a "suitable elementary education" at a place other than a State school. Section 18(2) of that Act provides that in a prosecution under this Act, the burden of proof that there is a reasonable excuse for the non-attendance of the child and that the child is receiving a suitable elementary education in some manner other than by attending a national or other suitable school rests on the person prosecuted. Best argued that such a provision was unconstitutional as the Act did not define what constitutes a "suitable elementary education".

Held: The Supreme Court found that the provision was constitutional. The burden was on Best to prove on a balance of probabilities that the children were receiving "suitable elementary education" at home. The Act needed to be interpreted and applied in a manner which respected the constitutionally guaranteed right of parents to educate their children in their home if that was their choice. The Act must also be interpreted to uphold the constitutional right of a child to receive a certain minimum education. *Director of Public Prosecutions v Christine Best; and Attorney-General, Notice Party* [2000] 2 I.R. 17.

Commentary
Rebuttable presumptions do appear in criminal law statutes—for example, where a person is arrested for possession of illegal drugs, and is carrying a quantity of drugs that appears too much for personal use, there might be a presumption created that he is a dealer rather than a user (see s.15(2) of the Misuse of Drugs Act 1977, as amended by the Misuse of Drugs Act of 1984). The possessor of the drugs would need to show that the quantity of drugs was for personal use only. In essence, therefore, a rebuttable presumption of law creates

an evidential burden. As the *Best* case demonstrates, this need only be rebutted on a balance of probabilities, despite it being in reply to a criminal charge.

JUDICIAL NOTICE

Judicial notice refers to a practice whereby a court can accept the truth of a fact without formal proof or evidence of that fact, on the ground that the fact is within the knowledge of the court itself.

This practice is an exception to the rule that a court is not entitled to decide disputed facts by reference to its own knowledge, but only to knowledge that has been put before it by the parties in the form of admissible evidence.

Key Principle: Judicial notice should only be taken of facts which are not in dispute. This avoids the delay and expense of taking evidence on issues that are "common cause".

Byrne v Londonderry Tramway Company [1902]

Byrne was travelling on the driver's platform of a tram when it derailed and he was thrown off, sustaining severe injury. Byrne sued the tram company on the basis of vicarious liability—in other words, he was claiming that the employer was responsible for the negligent acts of its employees within the scope of their employment.

Evidence was led that the tram drivers and conductors were under strict orders not to allow passengers to travel on the driver's platform, and there were signs on every tram forbidding the practice. Byrne's evidence was that the driver had allowed him to stand on the driver's platform, he did not see any sign forbidding the practice, and a sign had not been brought to his attention by the driver or a conductor.

Held: The tram company could not be held liable for Byrne's injuries as the driver was clearly acting outside the scope of his employment. The court accepted that it was not necessary to lead evidence as to what was done in the usual course of employment of tram drivers and tram conductors, as that was part of the "common knowledge of Judges and jurors". The court found that it was clearly not within the power of their employment for tram drivers or conductors to allow passengers to travel on a part of the car not constructed or intended for such purpose. *Byrne v Londonderry Tramway Company* [1902] 2 I.R. 457.

Key Principle: Judges have a wide discretion as to matters of which they will take judicial notice.

R. v Zundel (1987)

Ernst Zundel published a pamphlet denying that the Holocaust ever took place. He was charged in terms of s.181 of the Criminal Code of Canada with spreading false news which he knew to be false and which was likely to cause injury or mischief to the public interest.

On appeal, the prosecution argued that the trial judge was wrong in refusing to take judicial notice that the Holocaust did occur.

Held: The Ontario Court of Appeal upheld the trial judge's refusal to take judicial notice of the Holocaust. The effect of such a direction would have been an instruction to the jury that the fact of the Holocaust was so notorious as to be indisputable among reasonable persons. From that, they would have had to hold that Zundel knew that what he was publishing was false, and therefore the operation of judicial notice would have been gravely prejudicial to his defence against that charge.

The instruction to the jury did not prevent Zundel from putting forward his arguments as to the intention, mechanisms, scope and impact of the slaughter. He was still able to put forward his theory that the Holocaust was a fabrication and therefore the trial judge's instruction to the jury was legitimate. *Her Majesty the Queen v Ernst Zundel* (1987) 35 D.L.R. (4th) 338.

Commentary

The *Byrne* judgment might be criticised as it would seem that evidence as to what constituted the usual course of employment of tram drivers and tram conductors was the crux of this case. Clearly the judgment was based on the court's perception, rather than direct evidence, of what tram drivers and tram conductors could and could not do.

In the *Zundel* judgment the trial court was very careful in its instruction to the jury, stating that judicial notice could be taken of the fact that there was a mass murder and extermination of Jews in Europe by Nazis. The defendant's thesis was that whilst there were Jews killed in the war, six million did not die, and he further claimed that there was no official Nazi policy to exterminate Jews, and he finally claimed that the gas chambers were not built by the Nazis, but by the Russians after the war. Accordingly, the court was not taking judicial notice of any facts in dispute. If the court had gone further than it did, it would have compromised the defence of the accused, Ernst Zundel.

AUDI ALTERAM PARTEM

The literal interpretation of the phrase *audi alteram partem* is "hear the other side". What this means is that anyone whose rights, privileges and liberties are affected by the action of an administrative authority must be given an opportunity to be heard on the matter.

Key Principle: The principle of *audi alteram partem* has important implications for the procedural law of evidence as it means that the court must ensure that a person is allowed to both lead evidence and challenge evidence.

Keating v Crowley [2003]

An interim barring order in terms of the Domestic Violence Act of 1996 was made against David Keating after his wife had made an *ex parte* application (a hearing where only one party appears before the court in the absence of an opposing party, who is not notified of the hearing) to Judge Crowley in the District Court.

Keating unsuccessfully appealed this finding to the High Court, but was given leave by the High Court to apply to the Supreme Court by way of judicial review for a declaration that ss.1, 2 and 3 of the Act were unconstitutional.

One of the arguments put forward by Keating was that the provision allowing an *ex parte* application for a barring order was unconstitutional and violated the principle of *audi alteram partem* as it meant that a court could order a person from his own home without first hearing his version of events.

Held: The Supreme Court held that whilst the Oireachtas is entitled to limit the constitutional right of persons to due process in order to protect the constitutional rights of others, the extent of that limitation must be proportionate, and no more than is reasonably required in order to secure the constitutional right in question.

In the present case Keating was forcibly removed from his

family home, and faced arrest and possible criminal charges if he attempted to re enter his home once the order was made, all on the basis of unchallenged allegations. The Supreme Court declared that the provision in question was unconstitutional. *David Keating v Judge Timothy Crowley; and the Attorney-General; and the Director of Public Prosecutions; and Lorraine Keating (notice parties)* [2003] 1 I.L.R.M. 88.

Gill v Connellan [1988]

John Gill was convicted of drunken driving. He complained that his solicitor had great difficulty in cross-examining the arresting officer as the trial judge, Judge Connellan, continuously interrupted.

Held: A defendant should not be deprived of his basic rights of justice at a criminal trial such as the right to hear and test by examination the evidence offered by, or on behalf of, his accuser, to be allowed to give or call evidence in his defence and to be heard in argument or submission before judgment is given. The application for *certiorari* was granted. *John Gill v District Justice Peter A. Connellan* [1988] I.L.R.M. 448.

Key Principle: Article 38 of Bunreacht na hÉireann is the "due process" clause relating to criminal trials, as it says that no person shall be tried on any criminal charge save in the due course of law. Article 40.3 provides a similar right to fair procedures in civil trials, where a party is at risk of having his or her good name, person, property or personal rights jeopardised.

Borges v Medical Council [2004]

Sebastian Borges qualified to practise as a doctor in Ireland in 1974. He was also registered to practise in the United Kingdom. He originally practised in Cork, but left Ireland and practised in Scotland from 1994 to 1999. He was removed from the United Kingdom register of doctors after being found guilty of professional misconduct, namely inappropriate sexual conduct towards two female patients.

The Medical Council of Ireland wished to have the name of Dr Borges erased from the register of doctors in Ireland for the same offences, and instituted disciplinary proceedings against him. However, the two patients in question refused to give evidence to the council. The Medical Council decided that it would use the transcripts from the UK disciplinary hearing, where the two patients had testified and had been cross-examined.

Dr Borges protested that this violated his constitutional right to cross-examine the witnesses at the hearing in Ireland. The council responded by saying that the two patients had already been cross-examined and the other witnesses at the hearing in Ireland could be cross-examined.

Held: The Supreme Court found that where a tribunal is inquiring into an allegation of conduct which reflects on a person's good name or reputation, he or his lawyer must be allowed to cross-examine his accuser or accusers. *Sebastian Borges v the Fitness to Practise Committee of the Medical Council and the Medical Council* [2004] 2 I.L.R.M. 81.

2. Competence and Compellability of Witnesses

INTRODUCTION

Ordinarily, competence is the skill or knowledge to do something well. In the legal sense, competence means having the capacity or legal ability to do something. In the law of evidence, we say that a witness is competent if he or she may be called to give evidence in a court of law.

When somebody is compelled to do something, it means that they are doing that thing not as an exercise in free will, but because they have to, usually because of some external pressure or compulsion.

The same is true in the law of evidence. A witness is compellable when they can be forced to testify. Of course, the witness cannot be told what to say, but the witness can be sworn in and asked questions, and would face prosecution if they refused to answer any questions.

As a starting point it can be stated that all competent witnesses are compellable. However, there are some important exceptions to this rule.

Key Principle: Where the competence of a witness is challenged, the burden rests with the party calling that witness to prove that the witness is competent to testify in court. The question of competence is for the trial judge to determine.

Attorney-General v Kehoe [1951]

James Kehoe was charged with three counts of unlawful carnal knowledge of a woman of "feeble mind", in circumstances where it was clear that he knew that she was intellectually challenged. The prosecution tendered the testimony of the woman as evidence. The defence protested that the woman was not competent.

Held: The prosecution could examine the woman in order to demonstrate her competence. The defence could thereafter cross-examine the woman and lead evidence on the issue. The final issue of deciding the competency of the witness was for the judge alone. *The People (at the suit of the Attorney-General) v James Kehoe* [1951] I.R. 70.

Key Principle: The enquiry into the competence of a witness takes place in a separate hearing called the *voire dire*, where expert witnesses (for example, psychiatrists) are often called to testify about the mental competence of a proposed witness. The *voire dire* must take place in the absence of the jury.

DPP v Conroy [1986]

As a result of an investigation into a killing, Charles Conroy was brought to a Garda station and questioned. Whilst in custody, Conroy admitted to participating in the killing, and was charged with murder.

At the trial, the defence informed the judge that they intended to challenge the admissibility of Conroy's confession on a number of grounds. Counsel requested the trial judge to put these issues to the jury in accordance with the views expressed by the Supreme Court in *The People v Lynch* [1982] I.R. 64. The trial judge declined to leave the issue of the admissibility of the confession to the jury, and determined the matter in the jury's absence by *voire dire*. The trial judge ruled that the confession was admissible.

Conroy appealed to the Court of Criminal Appeal, arguing that the trial judge was wrong in not leaving the issue of admissibility to the jury. The Court of Criminal Appeal turned down the appeal, holding that the trial judge was not obliged to send every issue of admissibility to the jury. Conroy appealed this point to the Supreme Court.

Held: The Supreme Court found that the trial judge was correct in using the *voire dire*, in the absence of the jury, to determine the issue of the admissibility of evidence. To use the jury to determine this issue as a preliminary issue before the trial proper could inhibit the accused's counsel in his cross-examination of witnesses for the prosecution, who would be giving evidence in the trial proper, and could also result in prejudice on the part of the jury in determining the guilt or innocence of the accused. *The People (at the suit of the Director for Public Prosecutions) v Charles Conroy* [1986] I.R. 460.

Commentary

This was a controversial judgment. The Supreme Court was split on this issue and the slender majority opinion prevailed. The decision can be defended as the logical choice however, as the judge must decide questions of law, and the jury must decide questions of fact. A *voire dire* is designed to assess the admissibility of evidence, in this case a confession, as opposed to the truth of the content of that confession. Admissibility is a legal concept, not a factual concept, and it is, therefore, correct that the jury be sent out.

THE COMPETENCE OF CERTAIN CATEGORIES OF WITNESS

Children

Possibly as a result of the notoriety of the Salem Witch Trials and other more recent travesties, like *McMartin* and *Cleveland,* and the part that the testimony of children played in those proceedings, the common law has for a long time treated the evidence of children with deep suspicion.

In recent years, a great deal of research has been conducted on children and their testimonial competency, and the findings have demonstrated that, as long as children are properly interviewed and carefully questioned, their memories are as good as, and sometimes better, than adults'. A child's memory tends to be uncluttered, due to their short life experience and minimal responsibilities, and, accordingly, there is no reason why they should not be as competent on the witness stand as adults, if they are handled in a manner commensurate with their age and sensibilities.

Key Principle: There is no threshold age above which children are deemed to be competent or below which they are deemed incompetent. The competence of a child to give evidence is for the court to assess on an individual basis.

R. v Brasier (1779)

In a prosecution for indecent assault, the question arose whether a child under the age of seven years could give evidence.

Held: A child may be sworn in to testify at a criminal prosecution, provided that the child appears, on strict examination by the court, to possess a sufficient knowledge of the nature and consequences of the oath, there being no precise or fixed rule as to the time within which children are excluded from giving evidence. The admissibility of their evidence depends upon their appreciation of the danger of lying, and the importance of telling the truth, which is to be assessed according to the answers they give in reply to questions put to them by the court. *Rex v Brasier* (1779) 1 Leach C.C. 199; 168 E.R. 202.

Attorney-General v O'Sullivan [1930]

William O'Sullivan was convicted of sodomising a 10-year-old boy. The boy gave evidence that O'Sullivan had committed the offence. On appeal, O'Sullivan argued that the complainant, being a child under the age of 14 years, should not have been allowed to give evidence without preliminary examination as to his competence to give evidence on oath.

Held: The purpose of s.30 of the Children Act of 1908 was to enable a child "of tender years" who does not, in the opinion of the court, understand the nature of an oath, to give evidence not upon oath if, in the opinion of the court, the child has sufficient intelligence to justify the reception of the evidence and understands the duty of speaking the truth.

The section did not alter the law concerning the reception of the evidence of children given on oath which was, and is, a question, not of age, but of the intelligence and actual mental capacity of the child witness, and the child's ability to understand that it was wrong, and dangerous, to lie in a court of law.

Accordingly, the age of the child was not the sole determinant of competency. *Attorney-General v William O'Sullivan (1)* [1930] I.R. 553.

R. v Z. [1990]

Z. was convicted of incest with his five-year-old daughter. He argued in his appeal that the trial judge should not have allowed the evidence of such a young child.

Held: The Court of Appeal held that in the past the reluctance to accept the evidence of such young children was based, in part, on consideration for the child's feelings. With modern television and video-linked testimony, there should be a greater acceptance of the testimony of children. *R. v Z.* [1990] 2 Q.B. 355.

Commentary

In the past the test of competency for a child witness was whether the child understood the nature and consequences of the oath. Now that it is no longer necessary for a child to take the oath before testifying, the test is rather whether the child understands the difference between telling the truth and lying, and the importance of telling the truth to the court. Recently, there appears to be a shift from deciding a child's competence on the basis of reliability to deciding a child's competence on the basis of intelligibility (for example, s.27 of the Criminal Evidence Act of 1992 speaks of the child's capacity to give "an intelligible account of events"). In other words, as long as the evidence of the child can be understood, it should be received, and thereafter the weight of that evidence can be assessed as a matter of fact. This is more in keeping with the approach taken with adults.

Complainants in sexual offences cases

The common law was always suspicious about complainants in sexual offence cases, on the grounds that such complaints were easy to make up and difficult to refute. Under the common law it was obligatory for the trial judge to warn the jury of the need for caution when hearing the testimony of the complainant in a trial involving allegations of a sexual offence.

Key Principle: In trials involving complainants about sexual offences, s.7 of the Criminal Law (Rape) (Amendment) Act of 1990 now leaves it to the discretion of the trial judge whether to say anything to the jury about treating the evidence of the complainant with caution, and if the judge decides to say something, he or she has discretion concerning what to say, with the section stating that it is not necessary to use any "particular form of words".

R. v Makanjuola [1995]

Oluwanfunso Makanjuola was convicted of indecently assaulting the complainant by squeezing her breasts when they were alone together in a storeroom at their place of employment.

Makanjuola argued that the trial judge was wrong in failing to give any direction to the jury on corroboration and the need for caution.

Held: The appeal was dismissed with the Court of Appeal holding that there was no evidential basis for regarding the complainant as inherently unreliable. The case was straightforward and there was no reason for the judge to give any special warning. It is a matter for the judge's discretion whether any warning is necessary and appropriate. There must be an evidential basis for the warning, and not simply because the witness is a complainant in a sexual offence or is alleged to be an accomplice. Where the judge does give a warning, this must be as part of his general summing-up, and

not as a set-piece legal direction. The judge must decide on the
strength and terms of the warning. *R. v Oluwanfunso Makanjuola*
[1995] 1 W.L.R. 1348.

The intellectually challenged witness

Key Principle: The intellectually challenged witness is not
automatically disqualified from testifying. If the witness's disability
does not appear to affect his or her ability to understand what is
required and to communicate on a level that can be understood by
the jury, the court has the discretion to rule the witness competent.

DPP v T. (1988)

T. was charged with the rape and indecent assault of his daughter,
who testified for the prosecution. The girl had a mild form of Down's
Syndrome. The trial judge had asked her questions about her
understanding of the oath and the duty to tell the truth. The girl had
displayed sufficient knowledge of the human genitalia, assisted in
her testimony by anatomically correct dolls.

Held: The girl was declared competent to testify by the trial
judge, and this decision was upheld by the Court of Criminal Appeal.
*The People (at the suit of the Director for Public Prosecutions)
v T.* (1988) 3 Frewen 141.

Diplomats

By virtue of s.5(1) of the Diplomatic Relations Immunities Act of
1967, diplomatic agents and non-national members of administrative
and technical staff, as well as their non-national families, are
competent but not compellable to testify in an Irish court.

The accused

The accused is not competent as a prosecution witness, neither against
himself, nor, in a joint trial, against his co-accused. He is competent
but not compellable to give evidence in favour of another accused.

Key Principle: Even in instances where the accused are not tried
together in respect of the same crime, they cannot be compelled to
testify against one another.

Attorney-General v Ingham (1947)

A number of accused persons were charged on various counts of conspiracy. Information had been received against one of them and he was returned for trial in the Circuit Criminal Court. The prosecution wanted to call this accused as a witness against the others but they objected.

Held: A person charged with an indictable offence in the District Court was invested with a privilege which could not be impaired by compelling him to give evidence against a co-defendant during a preliminary enquiry before a judge into an alleged joint offence. The fact that he may have been committed for trial during the proceedings, while the co-defendant still awaited the issue of the justice's inquiry, did not affect his privilege. *Attorney-General v Ingham and Others* (1947) 82 I.L.T.R. 79.

Key Principle: If during separate trials (for the same offence) an accused pleads guilty and is convicted, the convicted person is then free to give evidence against the other accused. This evidence will be treated with caution, as the person who has pleaded guilty might feel some pressure to make his evidence favourable for the prosecution, in the hope that it will lead to him receiving a reduced sentence.

Attorney-General v Shribman and Samuels [1946]

Joseph Shribman and William Samuels were charged and convicted under the Emergency Powers Act of 1939, as amended by the Emergency Powers (Continuance and Amendment) Act of 1942, for exporting watches without a licence.

One of the issues taken on appeal was the trial court's reliance on the uncorroborated evidence of accomplice witnesses.

Held: The Court of Criminal Appeal held that the trial judge was entitled to act upon the uncorroborated evidence of accomplices, who had been convicted and were awaiting sentence, although it would have been more satisfactory if these witnesses had been sentenced before giving evidence. *The People (at the suit of the Attorney-General) v Joseph Shribman and William Samuels* [1946] I.R. 431.

Key Principle: If an accused person elects to testify in his own defence, he is making himself available for cross-examination by the prosecution and by the other accused in the trial, and he cannot argue that this offends his right of silence.

R. v Hilton [1972]

Keith Hilton was charged, and convicted with 10 others, with the offence of aiding and abetting an affray. The evidence was that a gang of between 20 and 40 youths in leather suits arrived on their motor cycles at a dance in a club in Bury; and proceeded to trash the premises and assault both men and women in the club.

During the trial one of Hilton's co-accused gave evidence in his own defence which did not incriminate any of the other accused, including Hilton. Hilton and the other co-accused applied to cross-examine the witness, but the trial judge ruled that, in the absence of any evidence by the witness tending to incriminate Hilton or any other accused, they had no right of cross-examination.

Hilton appealed his conviction, one of the grounds of appeal being the refusal of the judge to allow him to cross-examine his co-accused.

Held: The Court of Appeal upheld the appeal, and found that the ruling of the judge had been wrong. The right to cross-examine a co-defendant was well established and necessary in order that justice be done. Hilton's conviction was quashed. *R. v Keith Hilton* [1972] 1 Q.B. 421.

Commentary

Another scenario in which an accused is allowed to testify against a co-accused is where no evidence is offered against an accused and he is acquitted. The defence of *autrefois acquit* operates as a bar against possible subsequent prosecution and the individual concerned is free to testify against the other accused. *Autrefois acquit* means that if a person has been previously acquitted for an offence, he cannot be charged later with the same offence. In other words, new charges cannot be brought in relation to the same incident.

The spouse of the accused

Originally, the common law held that the spouse of an accused was not competent as a witness for the prosecution in a criminal trial.

The rule extended to a joint trial, so that even if the evidence of a spouse was only against the co-accused, that spouse could not testify. The rationale was derived from the rule that an accused cannot testify for the prosecution in a criminal trial. Historically, the husband and wife were regarded as one and so the spouse could not testify either.

Key Principle: One of the original justifications for marital privilege was the public policy ground of the need to protect the institution of marriage.

DPP v T. (1988)

T. was charged with the rape and indecent assault of his daughter. The child's mother, who was the wife of T., was called as a witness. T. objected to this and said that it was an attack on the institution of marriage for his wife to testify against him.

Held: The Court of Criminal Appeal found that the basis for the common law rule that spouses cannot testify against one another is that this would tend to rupture family relationships. However, this must be set against the public interest in the vindication of the innocent who may have been subjected to injustice. As both interests fell within the confines of Art.41, the interests of the innocent child must prevail. *The People (at the suit of the Director for Public Prosecutions) v T.* (1988) 3 Frewen 141.

Commentary
Largely as a result of the *T.* judgment, the Criminal Evidence Act of 1992 changed the common law dramatically. In criminal proceedings, the spouse (or former spouse) of an accused is:

- competent to give evidence for the prosecution, or for the accused, and a co-accused, concerning any offence;

- competent and compellable to give evidence at the instance of the accused; and

- competent and compellable to give evidence at the instance of the prosecution and a co-accused where the offence:

    ° involves violence or threatened violence to the spouse, a child of either spouse, or any person under the age of 17;

○   is a sexual offence against a child of either spouse or
    against any person under the age of 17.

The spouse of the accused is not competent to give evidence against
the other spouse, or compellable by the other spouse, where both
are charged with the same crime.

None of these provisions, however, affect any right of a spouse
or former spouse in respect of marital privacy. A former spouse
includes, in relation to the accused, a person who has been granted
a decree of divorce or of judicial separation or has entered into a
separation agreement.

3. Testimony of Witnesses

INTRODUCTION

Testimony or testimonial evidence is the evidence of a witness. Although people think of testimony as oral or spoken evidence only (*viva voce* evidence), in certain proceedings it is possible to have testimony on affidavit, which is a formal written statement made under oath.

The evidence of a witness in court is known as sworn evidence, because it is usually given under oath or affirmation. In certain defined circumstances, testimony may be given and admitted as unsworn evidence.

In general, however, all testimony must be made under oath, which is a solemn declaration where the witness calls on God to witness that what is said is true. At common law, the rule was that evidence had to be on oath in order to be admissible, and the moral aspect of the oath was emphasised, so much so that a person who had no religious belief would have been prohibited from testifying.

A secular alternative to the oath, the affirmation, was introduced into Irish law by the Oaths Act of 1888. Section 3 of the same Act provides that a person could take the oath despite not having a genuine religious belief, and that this would not affect the import of the oath or the admissibility of the evidence.

Key Principle: The fact that a person does not have any religious belief would not disqualify that person from taking the oath, as long as the court was satisfied that the importance of telling the truth was apparent to the witness and the witness regarded that obligation as binding on his or her conscience.

R. v Hayes [1977]

Three small boys, Martin, Trevor and George, aged 12, 11 and 9 respectively, were called to give evidence in a case of gross indecency.

Martin, the 12-year-old child, was asked by the trial judge if he had been given religious instruction. He replied in the negative. As a result of the trial judge's questions, it emerged that Martin did believe that there was a God, and he knew that it was bad and wicked to tell lies. As a result of this, he was sworn as a witness.

Held: The Court of Appeal confirmed that the important consideration when a judge has to decide whether a child should properly be sworn, is whether the child has sufficient appreciation of the solemnity of the occasion, and the added responsibility to tell the truth. The court pointed out that many adults would not recognise the divine sanction of the oath, but would still be permitted to testify under oath. *R. v Geoffrey Hayes* [1977] 2 All E.R. 288.

Key Principle: The critical issue is whether the witness appreciates the importance of telling the truth, and whether that witness takes that obligation seriously, or to put it another way, regards the obligation to tell the truth as binding on his or her conscience. Accordingly, the oath should not be restricted to any particular religion.

R. v Kemble [1990]

Peter Kemble was charged with possessing a firearm with intent to commit an offence. The main prosecution witness, Tareq Hijab, despite being a Muslim, took the oath on the New Testament.

Kemble appealed his conviction, arguing that Hijab did not regard the oath as binding on his conscience, as Muslims only believed in the Koran, and a Muslim had to take the oath on the Koran in Arabic.

Held: There was no reason that the oath should be restricted to those of the Jewish or Christian faith. What was important was that the oath taken appeared to the court to be binding upon the conscience of the witness and, secondly and most importantly, that the witness himself considered the oath to be binding upon his conscience. *R. v Peter Kemble* [1990] 3 All E.R. 116.

Key Principle: The failure to take the oath or solemn affirmation, even if such omission was in good faith and done inadvertently, renders the testimony useless and inadmissible, apart from instances where the law permits the taking of unsworn evidence.

R. v Marsham, Ex p. Pethick Lawrence [1912]

Emmeline Pethick Lawrence was charged with assaulting a police officer. Two police officers were called to give evidence for the prosecution. Lawrence did not lead any evidence. The magistrate convicted Lawrence and sentenced her to one month's imprisonment.

Later, on the same day, the magistrate's attention was drawn to the fact that one of the police officers had not been sworn when he gave his evidence. This was an innocent mistake. The magistrate thereafter reheard the charge, and the two police officers gave their evidence again, this time both under oath. On this occasion, Lawrence called witnesses, and they gave evidence (under oath). Lawrence was again convicted, and again sentenced to one month's imprisonment.

On review, Lawrence argued that the magistrate was *functus officio* after the first conviction, and could not hear the same charge twice and that, secondly, a person could not be charged with the same offence twice.

Held: As Lawrence was convicted on unsworn evidence, the first hearing was a mistrial, and accordingly was void, as if it had never happened. On this reasoning, the magistrate was not *functus officio*, as he had not discharged his office during the first hearing, and neither was Lawrence being charged with the same offence twice, as the first hearing was void. Therefore, at the time of the second hearing, she had not been convicted of that crime. *Rex v Marsham, Ex p. Emmeline Pethick Lawrence* [1911–13] All E.R. Rep. 639.

Commentary
Section 27 of the Criminal Evidence Act of 1992 allows a witness under the age of 14 years to give unsworn testimony if the court is satisfied that the child is capable of giving an intelligible account of events which are relevant to those proceedings.

This provision also applies to a witness, of any age, with an intellectual disability, subject to the same proviso—that the witness is capable of giving an intelligible account of events which are relevant to those proceedings.

This is an express departure from the common law.

Key Principle: The concept of testimony has now been broadened through advances in technology, for example, evidence by video-link. A consequence of this is that the right of a person to confront his or her accuser is satisfied by what is essentially a confrontation of the minds. It is not necessary to physically confront your accuser to satisfy the right.

Donnelly v Ireland [1998]

Anthony Donnelly was charged with sexually assaulting a 14-year-old girl. Despite objections by the defence at the time, the complainant was allowed to give her evidence through video link. Donnelly was convicted and sentenced to five years' imprisonment.

Donnelly took his conviction on review to the High Court and argued that the giving of evidence by live television link was unconstitutional because it prevented the accused from confronting his accuser, and further breached the requirement that the evidence against an accused must be given in his presence.

The High Court dismissed Donnelly's application for review and Donnelly appealed this decision to the Supreme Court, using the same arguments.

Held: The Supreme Court held that the right to confrontation does not depend upon the physical presence of the witness in the court. The rights of the accused were protected by requiring the witness to be cross-examined via live television link so that the court and the parties before the court could observe the demeanour of the witness and listen to the verbal responses of the witness in the usual way. *Anthony Donnelly v Ireland* [1998] 1 I.R. 321.

ELICITATION OF TESTIMONY

When you elicit something, you seek it out in order to obtain it. The elicitation of evidence concerns the recognised and approved methods of getting the testimony out of the witness and into court.

Language

Key Principle: A witness is entitled to give evidence in any language. The proviso to this entitlement is that, if necessary, the testimony of that witness must be interpreted so that all the parties involved in the case can understand the testimony.

Ó'Monacháin v An Taoiseach [1986]

Tomás Ó'Monacháin was charged in the District Court at Bunbeg, a Gaeltacht area, for contravening the Local Government Act of 1963 in that he used the land for a caravan and a mobile home without the necessary licence.

Ó'Monacháin elected to conduct his trial in Irish. The judge accordingly appointed an interpreter. Ó'Monacháin objected, arguing that the judge did not seem to have sufficient Irish which would put him at a disadvantage. He asked the judge to recuse himself and adjourn the matter until a judge with sufficient Irish could be appointed. The trial judge refused and proceeded to hear the case with the help of an interpreter. Ó'Monacháin was convicted in the District Court. This was confirmed by the High Court and he appealed his conviction to the Supreme Court.

Held: The Supreme Court rejected the appeal and confirmed the conviction. The court held that there was no obligation on a district justice to hear a case without an interpreter. If a district judge is appointed to a district where Irish is in general use, he must be competent under s.71 of the Courts Act of 1974 to function with the help of an interpreter when evidence is given in Irish. An accused or a witness has the right to give evidence in Irish but an accused under s.71 cannot force a judge to hear a case completely in Irish if there is a witness or anybody else partaking in the case that does not understand Irish. *Tomás Ó'Monacháin v An Taoiseach, An tAire Leasa Shóisialaigh, An tAire Airgeadis, An tAire Dlí agus Ciret, An tAire Sláinte, An tAire Gnóthaí Eachtracha, An tAire Talamhaíochta, An tAire Tionscail, Aire na Gaeltachta, An tAire Oideachais, An tAire Cosanta, An tAire Poist agus Telegrafa, Aire na Seirbhíse Poiblí, An tAire Iompair agus Cumhachta, An tAire Tailte, An tAire Rialtais Áitiúil, an Breithheamh Dúiche Patrick Keenan Johnson, an Breitheamh Dúiche Michael Larkin agus An tArd-Aighne* [1986] I.L.R.M. 660.

Examination-in-chief

When you question your own witness for the first time in court, this is known as the examination-in-chief. A leading question is a question that implies or suggests or even contains an answer. As a general rule, the lawyer conducting an examination-in-chief is not allowed to ask leading questions of his or her own witness.

Key Principle: A witness can be declared hostile by the court where it appears that the witness is contradicting earlier testimony given or where that witness is refusing to answer questions. If the court agrees to declare a witness hostile, this means that the lawyer is allowed to cross-examine his or her own witness, in other words, ask leading questions.

Attorney-General v Taylor [1974]

Taylor was convicted of murder after stabbing the deceased. The wife of the deceased had made a written statement that the weapon used was a knife, whereas in her testimony she gave evidence that the weapon was a pair of scissors. After the jury was removed, counsel for the prosecution applied to have her declared a hostile witness, and the application was granted by the judge. When the jury returned, counsel proceeded to cross-examine his own witness by referring to her earlier statement. The witness was never asked which version was the true version (scissors or knife) and it was clear that counsel was attempting to undermine her credibility.

Taylor appealed his conviction, arguing that the procedure used in declaring the witness hostile was faulty.

Held: The proper procedure was for the prosecution to put her previous statement to the witness and if she denied that, have her stand down, and take the evidence of the person who took the statement, proving it in the ordinary way without revealing the contents at that stage. The original witness should then have been returned to the stand and after identifying her statement now before the court, she should have been asked to comment on the discrepancy. If she continued to deny the contradiction, then the statement, having been already proved, could have gone in as evidence of the fact that the witness had made a contrary statement. It should have been made clear to the jury that what the witness said in her written statement is not evidence of its content but is only evidence on the question of whether or not she had said something else—it was evidence going to her credibility. *The People (at the suit of the Attorney-General) v Taylor* [1974] I.R. 97.

Cross-examination

Cross-examination is the process by which counsel questions the witnesses of the opposing party, after they have completed the examination-in-chief.

There are two main objects of cross-examination. These are to cast doubt on the version which has been presented in examination-in-chief and, in so doing, undermine the credibility of that witness; and secondly, to get the witness to confirm the evidence presented or to be presented by the opposing witnesses, and also to agree with the conclusions and inferences that the opposing party seeks to draw from the evidence.

Cross-examination may, therefore, focus both on the credibility of the witness and on the facts in dispute. As a general rule, it can be said that counsel can ask anything in cross-examination, subject of course to the principle of relevance. The most important exception to this general rule is what is known as the collateral issue rule.

Key Principle: A witness may be asked questions during cross-examination that suggest that the witness is mistaken or lying. These questions are challenging the credibility of a witness, rather than challenging the facts contained in the testimony. However, the cross-examiner may not produce evidence to prove that the witness is lying where the matter is not directly relevant to the facts in issue, and the only thing at stake is the credibility of the witness. These matters are said to be collateral to the facts in issue, and a witness's answers in reply to such questions are treated as final.

Attorney-General v Hitchcock **(1847)**

A witness by the name of Spooner was asked under cross-examination whether he had previously said that the officers of the Crown had offered him a bribe to give evidence against the accused. Spooner denied that he had ever said so. The cross-examining lawyer asked the Court to allow evidence to be led that Spooner had indeed made such a statement.

Held: Evidence to show that the witness had indeed made such a statement was inadmissible if it was for the purpose of affecting the credibility of the witness. The question was irrelevant to the issue, and raised a collateral issue. *Attorney-General v Hitchcock* (1847) 1 Exch. 91.

Key Principle: There are exceptions to the collateral evidence rule. One is allowed to lead evidence to rebut answers on collateral issues where the witness has made a previous inconsistent statement, or where the witness denies having a previous conviction, or where the witness denies that he or she is biased, or where there is medical evidence to suggest that the witness is unreliable due to a physical or intellectual disability.

Toohey v Metropolitan Police Commissioner [1965]

Brian Toohey and two others were charged with assaulting with intent to rob a youth of 17 in an alley. The youth gave evidence that Toohey had dragged him into the alley and assaulted him, and thereafter had searched his pockets.

Two police officers testified that they had come upon the youth and the three accused, with the youth in a distressed and hysterical condition.

Toohey testified in his defence that they had come upon the youth who appeared to have been drinking, was behaving very strangely, and seemed incapable of taking care of himself. The three accused had decided to take the youth home, but he had become hysterical and had banged himself against a wall, claiming that they were after his money.

The police surgeon who examined the youth at the police station testified that there were no bruises or signs of injury on the youth, that he smelt strongly of alcohol and that, throughout the examination, he was weeping and in an hysterical state.

The trial judge ruled that it was inadmissible to ask the surgeon any further questions about the role that alcohol played in the youth's state or whether he was more prone to hysteria than an ordinary person.

Toohey was convicted by the Central Criminal Court. He appealed to the Court of Criminal Appeal which dismissed his appeal. Despite the fact that the Court of Criminal Appeal had rejected Toohey's leave to appeal to the House of Lords, the Lords granted him leave to appeal.

Held: The House of Lords held that the evidence was admissible as it was relevant to the facts in issue, namely, did the assault take place or was it a figment of the youth's hysteria? Secondly, medical evidence is admissible to show that a witness suffers from some disease, or defect, or abnormality of the mind that affects the reliability of his or her evidence, and such evidence is not confined to a general opinion of the unreliability of the witness, but may give consideration to all the matters necessary to show not only the foundations of, and reasons for, the diagnosis, but also the extent to which the credibility of the witness is affected. Toohey's conviction was quashed. *Brian Anthony Toohey v Metropolitan Police Commissioner* [1965] 1 All E.R. 506.

Re-examination

Re-examination is the third phase of the questioning of a witness, and consists of questions asked by the lawyer that originally called that witness to testify.

New evidence may not be led during re-examination. Questions must be confined to dealing with evidence that was introduced either during examination-in-chief or that arose during cross-examination. Essentially re-examination can be used to emphasise favourable points that arose during examination-in-chief and perhaps cross-examination, and to attempt to repair any damage caused to the witness during cross-examination.

Using notes to refresh your memory

Where a witness uses notes (which must be made at the time of, or immediately after, the incident in question) whilst under oath and giving testimony, these notes form part of the testimony.

However, where a witness refreshes his or her memory by reading the notes before taking the oath, and does not use the notes during the testimony, the notes themselves become hearsay.

Key Principle: When a witness is allowed to read his or her statement before testifying, it is proper to inform the opposing counsel that this has occurred.

R. v Westwell [1976]

Stephen Westwell was charged with assault after being in a fight. Statements were taken from a number of witnesses at the time. The trial took place 11 months after the incident. Before the trial began, certain prosecution witnesses asked if they could see their written statements and they were allowed to do so. The prosecution did not inform the defence that this had been done. The defence discovered this before the close of the prosecution case.

Westwell asked the judge to direct the jury to acquit because of this. The judge refused and Westwell was convicted. He appealed his conviction to the Court of Appeal.

Held: The Court of Appeal found that there was no rule prohibiting witnesses from seeing their statements at the time of trial. If the prosecution was aware that witnesses had seen their statements before giving evidence, it would be appropriate to inform the defence, but their failure to do so could not of itself be a ground for appeal. The court had to consider whether such failure meant that the trial could not be continued without some prejudice or risk of injustice to the defendant. Westwell had not been prejudiced because he had known that the witnesses had seen their statements before the close of the prosecution case, and it was open to him to recall those witnesses and to make any appropriate points abut the weight to be attached to their evidence. *R. v Stephen Westwell* [1976] 2 All E.R. 812.

THE RULE AGAINST NARRATIVE

The rule against narrative prohibits the admission into evidence of statements made by a witness before the trial, where those statements are consistent with the testimony of the witness. This is based on the logical premise that the truthfulness or untruthfulness of a statement does not change through repetition.

Key Principle: The fact that a witness has made a statement more than once is irrelevant and inadmissible.

R. v Roberts [1942]

Frederick Roberts was charged with the murder of his former girlfriend, Nina Woods, by shooting her with a service rifle, after she had left him for another man. His defence was that the death had been an accident. He sought to lead evidence that he had a conversation with his father two days after the deceased was shot, in which he mentioned that his defence would be based on accident.

Held: As the remark made by Roberts to his father was not contemporaneous with the shooting incident, it was inadmissible. The rule against narrative precluded either the accused or his father referring to the conversation during their respective testimonies. *R. v Frederick Thomas Roberts* [1942] 1 All E.R. 187.

Key principle: An important exception to the rule against narrative is a complaint in a sexual offence case, where it is shown that the complaint is made voluntarily and at the first reasonable opportunity after the commission of the alleged offence.

DPP v Brophy [1992]

Robert Brophy was convicted on a charge of indecent assault on a 14-year-old girl in Dublin Circuit (Criminal) Court and was sentenced to five years' imprisonment.

Brophy owned a shop and it was alleged that he offered to make pendulums for the complainant and her friend at his house. He drove the girl to his house where it was alleged that the sexual assault took place.

Evidence was given by a security guard at the shopping centre that the girl had got out of Brophy's car, without any signs of distress, and had said to him: "I'll see you tomorrow." The complainant travelled to her mother's house, where she stayed for some time, but made no complaint. Thereafter she met up with three girl friends and spent time with them before she met with her father. Evidence was led that the complainant was in a distressed state when she met with her friends and later when she met with her father.

Held: The Court of Criminal Appeal held that the fact of the complaint was not admissible as it had not been made at the first reasonable opportunity. Complaints may only be proved in criminal prosecutions for a sexual offence, and must not be seen as evidence of the truth of the complaint, but rather that a complaint was made.

The Court held that this was not a case in which to exercise its discretion to order a re-trial, as, apart from the questionable evidence, no court would be justified in the circumstances of this case in imposing any further sentence of imprisonment on the appellant, who had already served one year's imprisonment on the charge. *The People (at the suit of the Director of Public Prosecutions) v Robert Brophy* [1992] 1 I.L.R.M. 709.

Commentary

What is important in this exception to the rule against narrative is the fact that the statement was made contemporaneously with the incident or as close to the incident as reasonably possible. In *Roberts* the statement by Roberts to his father did not fall within this exception as it was made a while after the shooting.

In sexual offences, to fall within the exception, the complaint must be made at the first opportunity. Such evidence is admissible to show the consistency of the complaint and therefore enhances the credibility of the complainant. It cannot be regarded as corroboration of the complainant's evidence, as it does not come from a source that is independent of the complainant's evidence.

This principle of contemporaneousness is similar to the other exceptions to the rule against narrative, namely allowing evidence of a previous identification (as long as it is made soon after the incident) and allowing statements which are inherently linked with the incident (*res gestae*).

The other exception to the rule is that a witness may admit evidence of previous consistent statements where it is alleged that his or her testimony is invented after the incident in question.

4. Corroboration

Certain types of evidence have traditionally been regarded as unreliable. Whether this perception is justified is a matter of continuing controversy.

One of the ways in which this seemingly unreliable evidence is "made safe" is by corroboration. The ordinary meaning of corroborate is to confirm, support or endorse. In the law of evidence, the word has a slightly more technical and extended meaning, but the principle is the same.

Key Principle: Corroboration is independent evidence which confirms that the accused person is connected with the crime in the sense that it confirms not only that a crime has been committed, but that it was the accused person who committed it.

As the finders of fact in a criminal trial, the jury must be warned about the dangers of uncorroborated evidence. The nature and severity of the warning is at the discretion of the judge.

Attorney-General v Williams [1940]

Denis Williams was charged with having unlawful carnal knowledge of a girl under the age of 15 years. He was found guilty and sentenced to five years' imprisonment.

The evidence by the complainant was that Williams had raped her whilst they were together gathering firewood. She had not complained to anyone on their return to the house and the allegations against Williams were only made by the complainant when she was discovered to be pregnant and later had a child.

Williams denied these allegations.

In his instructions to the jury, the trial judge told the jury that the question they were to decide was whether they believed the complainant beyond a reasonable doubt or whether they believed Williams, and that the accused was entitled to the benefit of any reasonable doubt that they might have.

The trial judge did not direct the jury's attention to the fact that the evidence of the complainant was uncorroborated, nor did he caution the jury that they should consider the evidence with particular care in view of her age and the nature of the charges.

Williams argued on appeal that the judge had failed to point out that the complainant's evidence was uncorroborated, and that he had failed to alert the jury to the dangers of uncorroborated evidence. His application for leave to appeal was refused by both the trial court and the Court of Criminal Appeal, but the latter court did refer the matter on appeal to the Supreme Court as involving a point of law of exceptional public importance.

Held: The Supreme Court held that the attention of the jury should have been directed by the trial judge to the absence of corroboration and a warning should have been given to the jury of the necessity of exercising great care in weighing the evidence of the complainant. The degree and gravity of the warning should depend upon the particular circumstances of the case, but in every case, when an adequate warning has been given, the jury should be told that they are entitled to act on the evidence of the complainant if they are satisfied beyond all reasonable doubt that it is truthful. *The People (at the suit of the Attorney-General) v Denis Williams* [1940] I.R. 195.

Commentary
This decision followed and confirmed the English decision of *R. v Baskerville* [1916] 2 K.B. 658, which had formulated the classic definition of corroboration:

> "We hold that evidence in corroboration must be independent testimony which affects the accused by connecting or tending to connect him with the crime. In other words, it must be evidence which implicates him, that is, which confirms in some material particular not only the evidence that the crime has been committed, but also that the prisoner committed it."

Key Principle: In order to qualify as evidence that corroborates the testimony of a witness, that evidence must come from a source that is independent of the witness.

DPP v P.C. **[2002]**

P.C. was charged with unlawful sexual intercourse with a young girl. The prosecution alleged that he met the complainant outside her school and drove her to his house, where he had sexual intercourse with her in his bedroom. The complainant had given evidence describing his bedroom.

After giving the jury the required corroboration warning, the trial judge proceeded to instruct the jury that the complainant's description of the windows and curtains in P.C.'s bedroom could be regarded as corroboration of her evidence.

Held: The Court of Criminal Appeal held that this evidence was not corroboration of the complainant's testimony as it was not independent of her testimony. *The People (at the suit of the Director of Public Prosecutions) v P.C.* [2002] 2 I.R. 285.

Key Principle: In certain circumstances, the accused might provide the corroborating evidence.

R. v Lucas [1981]

Iyabode Ruth Lucas was convicted of importing cannabis into England in contravention of the Customs and Excise Act 1952 and the Misuse of Drugs Act 1971.

The evidence was that Lucas faced two counts, after being caught with 25.17 kilograms of cannabis at Gatwick Airport on December 12, 1978, and thereafter being caught with 18.12 kilograms of cannabis at Heathrow Airport on February 7, 1979.

One of the grounds of appeal was that the trial judge had directed the jury that they could consider the lies told by the accused during her testimony as being corroborative of the testimony of an accomplice witness, a man called Crike Areh, who had pleaded guilty to the Gatwick offence and was sentenced to 18 months' imprisonment. Lucas argued that this was a misdirection.

Held: Lies told by an accused person (whether in or out of court) can provide corroboration for the evidence of an accomplice witness where it is determined that the lie was deliberate, that the lie related to a material issue, that the motive for the lie must be a realisation of guilt and a fear of the truth and it must be clearly shown that the statement or testimony by the accused is a lie by reference to evidence other than that of the testimony of the accomplice. The lies of the accused could have corroborated the testimony of an independent witness.

The appeal was upheld in respect of the Gatwick offence, and the sentence of two years' imprisonment was quashed. However, the sentence of three years' imprisonment for the Heathrow offence was confirmed. *R. v Lucas (Ruth)* [1981] 3 W.L.R. 121 (C.A.)

Commentary

The decision in *Lucas* has not yet been explored or applied in Ireland, but there is no reason to believe that the Irish courts will not follow the same logic.

At the same time, and somewhat controversially, there is Irish legislation which provides that the silence of the accused, when asked to co-operate (the taking of samples, for example) or for an explanation, or a failure to mention facts later relied on in his defence, can amount to corroboration. For example, ss.18 and 19 of the Criminal Justice Act of 1984 provide that where an accused person is asked by an investigating officer to explain certain objects in his or her possession or his or her presence in a particular place, and the accused refuses or fails to provide an explanation, this can be taken as corroborating evidence, although a conviction may not be based solely upon the inferences drawn from this corroborating evidence.

Key Principle: The corroborating evidence must implicate the accused in the commission of the crime.

James v R. (1971)

James was charged in Jamaica with raping a young woman, Elsada Hall. The complainant gave evidence that James had threatened her with a gun and a knife, taken her back to her room, and raped her.

Evidence was led that when James was confronted by the complainant, and later by the police, he did not attempt to flee, willingly gave his name and address, and denied knowing the complainant. His words at the time were: "No, no, you must be a mad woman, for is the first time I see you," and turning to the police officer, he said, "Officer, this girl tek me for the wrong person yah sah. Me sleep a me bed whole night." There was no trace of a gun or a knife on his premises. He did not have a pair of boots as the complainant had described them. An examination of his trousers did not reveal that he had recently had sexual intercourse in them, although the complainant had testified that her attacker had left his pants on when he raped her.

Forensic evidence was led that the complainant had had sexual intercourse at the time of the alleged incident. When directing the jury with regard to the evidence, the judge directed the jury that they were entitled to regard the evidence as corroboration of the complaint. James was convicted, and sentenced to 10 years' hard labour, and 12 strokes.

The conviction was appealed to the Court of Appeal, on the grounds that the judge had misdirected the jury. James was granted leave to appeal, but the sentence of corporal punishment was thereafter carried out. The appeal was heard a year after the conviction, and was turned down, with the Court of Appeal finding that the directions of the trial judge were "adequate".

James further appealed the matter to the Privy Council, and again this was heard a year later, almost two years after his conviction.

Held: The Privy Council held that the evidence had only confirmed that the complainant, Elsada Hall, had had sexual intercourse. It did not establish that it was James who had penetrated her, nor did it establish that the intercourse was without her consent. As such, it did not implicate James in the commission of an offence, and therefore was not corroborative evidence. The appeal was upheld and the conviction quashed, with the Privy Council expressing its shock at the fact that James was lashed despite having been given leave to appeal. *James v R.* (1971) 55 Cr.App.R. 299.

Key Principle: Although the corroborating evidence is usually direct evidence that is independent of the testimony of the complainant, there is no reason why the corroborating evidence cannot be an aggregate of circumstantial evidence, as long as the circumstantial evidence is independent of the complainant's testimony.

DPP v Reid [1993]

Paul Reid was charged and convicted for rape. The evidence was that he had picked up the complainant at a bus stop, brought her back to his house, and raped her, both vaginally and orally. His defence was that she had willingly accompanied him back to his house and there was consensual sex. He denied that there was any oral sex.

The prosecution argued that there were a number of pieces of evidence that could be regarded as corroboration:

- the medical evidence was that the intercourse had been accompanied by a considerable amount of force, although there was no evidence of other assault or injury;

- the evidence of the parents and the Gardaí was that the complainant was in a distressed condition after the incident;

- the evidence of the Gardaí was that the volume of the television set in the defendant's living room had been set at a very loud level, the supposition being that this was designed to drown out any cries of distress; and

- when woken up, the defendant had denied leaving his house all evening, such statement being later contradicted by his own testimony.

The trial judge did deliver the standard corroboration warning to the jury, and Reid was convicted by the jury. Reid appealed his conviction on the grounds that the judge should have laid greater stress on the dangers of convicting in the absence of corroboration and that he had given no assistance to the jury as to what items of evidence might constitute corroboration, and on that basis the jury might have approached the matter in the belief that the above-mentioned evidence did constitute corroboration.

Held: The Court of Criminal Appeal confirmed that the warning to the jury did not have to take any particular form. The court was satisfied that the judge had adequately warned the jury. The court found that the four items of evidence described above as supporting the prosecution were all matters which were independent of the complainant's own evidence and which could, in the view of the jury, have tended to confirm the account of the complainant. The conviction was confirmed. *The People (at the suit of the Director of Public Prosecutions) v Paul Reid* [1993] 2 I.R. 186.

Commentary

This decision is often cited in support of the argument that Irish law has moved away from the strictness of the original corroboration test laid down by the *Baskerville* decision, which was followed by the Supreme Court in *People v Williams*, discussed earlier in this chapter.

In essence the court was taking the four items of evidence as a whole, rather than singly, and finding that the inference created by the aggregate of this evidence was sufficient to constitute corroboration of the complaint. It is doubtful whether any item of evidence on its own could have constituted telling corroboration. This is a more realistic approach, and is consistent with the approach taken with circumstantial evidence, where the cumulative effect of the evidence is the critical factor.

At the same time, it might be argued that such an approach was contemplated by *Baskerville*. At page 367 of that judgment, Reading L.C.J. held that:

> "The corroboration need not be direct evidence that the accused committed the crime; it is sufficient if it is merely circumstantial evidence of his connection with the crime."

THE NEED FOR CORROBORATION

The requirement of independent proof was originally applied to witnesses who traditionally required their testimony to be corroborated, and as such these witnesses were not allowed to corroborate each others' testimony. This rule has been progressively relaxed in regard to the testimony of complainants in cases of sexual assault and the testimony of children, but has been maintained in the case of accomplice witnesses. In essence, it is probably more accurate to say that when it comes to the former categories of witness, the court will look for evidence that supports, as opposed to corroborates, the testimony of those witnesses. However, the danger of accomplice evidence is more apparent, and the requirement remains in regard to their evidence.

Key Principle: An accomplice is a person who assists the accused in the commission of an offence. Therefore, it would seem that the definition of accomplice must be decided in relation to the specific offence being tried.

Davies v DPP [1954]

Michael Davies was a member of a gang who attacked another gang. During the ensuing fight a member of the opposing gang was fatally stabbed.

Originally, all six of the gang members were charged with murder, but at the trial the prosecution offered no evidence against the other five gang members and they were acquitted.

Davies now stood alone on a charge of murder. At his trial, one of his fellow gang members testified against him, with the evidence being that Davies had admitted to using the knife. The trial judge did not warn the jury against the dangers of receiving the uncorroborated evidence of the witness.

Davies argued that the witness was an accomplice witness and, accordingly, the trial judge should have warned the jury.

Held: The definition of accomplice has to be decided in relation to the crime charged. The accused was charged with murder and therefore the definition of accomplice had to be determined in relation to the crime of murder. The witness was not an accomplice to murder as there was no evidence that the witness knew that any of his fellow gang members carried a knife and therefore the prosecution would not have been able to prove that he intended the attack with the knife to occur. *Michael John Davies v Director of Public Prosecutions* [1954] A.C. 378.

DPP v Kilbourne [1973]

John Kilbourne was charged with committing sex offences against young boys. In a strict sense, the boys were "accomplices" to the crime of buggery, and as such their evidence required corroboration.

Kilbourne was charged on an indictment containing seven counts, and was convicted of one offence of buggery, one of attempted buggery and five of indecent assault. The counts fell into two groups. Counts 1 to 4 referred to offences alleged to have been committed in 1970 and involved four boys; counts 5 to 7 alleged that the offences committed in 1971 involved two other boys. The boys were all between the ages of 9 and 12 at the time of the alleged offences.

Kilbourne admitted that the boys were in his house at various times, but claimed that the activities in the house were purely innocent, with the boys helping to spread word in the community about his business as a painter and decorator.

The trial judge directed the jury that, whereas the boys in each of the two groups knew each other well and could have collaborated in putting forward their stories, it was unlikely, if not impossible, for the two groups to have collaborated in that way and, accordingly, they were entitled to take the evidence of the boys in one group as corroborating the evidence of the boys in the other group. The jury returned a verdict of guilty.

The Court of Appeal quashed the convictions holding that, although the evidence of the boys of one group was admissible in relation to charges concerning boys of the other group as tending to show that Kilbourne was a homosexual whose sexual activities took a particular form and as tending to rebut the defence of innocent association, that evidence could not in law constitute corroboration of the evidence of boys of the other group. The prosecution appealed this finding to the House of Lords.

Held: The House of Lords held that the evidence of the 1970 complainants could corroborate the evidence of the 1971 complainants. The word "corroboration" had no special technical meaning; by itself, it meant no more than evidence tending to confirm other evidence. No distinction could, therefore, be drawn between evidence which could be used as corroboration and evidence which might help the jury to determine the truth of the matter. Since the evidence of one group of boys was admissible in relation to the charges concerning the other group as being relevant to matters in dispute and implicating the accused in the criminal conduct alleged, that evidence, if believed, constituted corroboration. It was immaterial that the evidence of boys of both groups was mutually corroborative, or that each boy was, technically, an accomplice in relation to the offence committed against him. *Director of Public Prosecutions v John Kilbourne* [1973] A.C. 729.

Key Principle: The approach of the Irish courts to the definition of an accomplice witness is wider than the original approach of the English courts. An accomplice can be defined as anyone implicated in the crime, either as a principal or accessory to the crime charged.

Attorney-General v Carney and Mulcahy **[1955]**

Henry Carney and Patrick Mulcahy were convicted of receiving stolen goods, and their conviction rested largely on the evidence of an accomplice witness, John Kelly, whose van was used in the theft, and whose garage and garden were used to hide the stolen goods.

On appeal it was argued that the trial judge should have decided that the witness was an accomplice and given an absolute corroboration warning, rather than leaving it for the jury to decide.

Held: The majority of the Supreme Court held that a very slight degree of complicity, either as principal or accessory in the crime charged, is sufficient to render a person an accomplice for the rule. *The People (at the suit of the Attorney-General) v Henry Carney and Patrick Mulcahy (1)* [1955] I.R. 324.

Commentary

It is important to realise that Irish law has not undergone all of the statutory changes which have occurred in English law. In England, s.34(2) of the Criminal Justice Act of 1988 and s.32(1) of the Criminal Justice and Public Order Act of 1994 have abolished the requirement that the trial judge gives a full corroboration warning merely because the witness is a child, or a complainant in a sexual offence trial, or an accomplice.

In Ireland, s.7 of the Criminal Law (Rape) Amendment Act of 1990 leaves the matter of a corroboration warning to the discretion of the trial judge when instructing the jury in a trial involving a sexual offence complaint, whilst s.28 of the Criminal Evidence Act of 1992 abolished the corroboration requirement for unsworn testimony, and the mandatory corroboration warning for sworn testimony by child witnesses.

However, with regard to accomplice witnesses, there has not been a similar statutory amendment, and Irish law is still governed by the strict common law requirement of a mandatory and full corroboration warning when the jury are instructed about the testimony of accomplice witnesses.

Key Principle: Legislation has been introduced to make certain warnings on corroboration discretionary, in other words, to be decided by the trial judge. These warnings were regarded by the common law as practices that had acquired the rule of law, and were therefore mandatory. The legislation has retained the warnings, but made them discretionary in regard to certain kinds of witnesses, most importantly complainants in sexual offence cases and children.

DPP v J.E.M. [2001]

J.E.M. was found guilty on each of four counts of sexual assault on a 15-year-old girl. He was sentenced to an effective two years' imprisonment.

One of the grounds of appeal was that the trial judge was wrong in his refusal to give the jury a warning that it was dangerous for them to convict the accused in the absence of corroboration, and that, furthermore, it was wrong for the trial judge to tell the jury that defence counsel was wrong for saying in his summing up that it was dangerous to convict in the absence of corroboration in a trial for a sexual offence.

Held: The Supreme Court held that s.7 of the Criminal Law
(Rape)(Amendment) Act of 1990 was quite clear in stating that it
is for the judge to decide in his discretion, having regard to the
evidence, whether the jury should be given a warning about the
danger of convicting the accused on the uncorroborated evidence
of the complainant. Whereas the wording of the legislation in
England and Wales was not exactly the same as the wording in the
Irish statute, the underlying policy and the legal principle underlying
both statutes was similar. The approach taken by the Court of
Appeal in *R. v Makanjuola* [1995] 1 W.L.R. 1348 was endorsed.
This approach was that there should be an evidential basis for the
warning (for example, where the quality of the witness's evidence
was unsatisfactory), and it should not be given solely on the basis
that the case involved a sexual offence. It is for the judge to decide
if there should be a warning at all, and if there is to be one, it is for
the judge to decide the strength and terms of that warning. The
Court of Appeal will only interfere with a trial judge's exercise of
his or her discretion where that exercise is unreasonable. *The
People (at the suit of the Director of Public Prosecutions) v
J.E.M.* [2001] 4 I.R. 385.

Key Principle: The witness in the witness protection programme
("the grass") is still an accomplice witness and can be treated as
such. The trial judge must give a warning to the jury about the dangers
of relying on such evidence without corroboration. Once the warning
is given, the jury can determine the appropriate weight to be attached
to such evidence and can convict in the absence of corroborative
evidence.

DPP v Gilligan [2005]

John Gilligan was convicted by the Special Criminal Court of drug
offences. The principal evidence against Gilligan came from previous
accomplices of his who were in the witness protection programme.
Gilligan argued that the witnesses were receiving special benefits
under the programme and this would be the motive for those witnesses
to lie. He was convicted and the conviction was confirmed by the
Court of Criminal Appeal. However, that Court certified two points
of law of exceptional public importance for the determination of the
Supreme Court.

The questions were as follows:

* In what circumstances and to what extent is evidence which may have been obtained from witnesses under a state Witness Protection Programme inadmissible and/or inconsistent with trial in due course of law as guaranteed by Art.38.1 of the Constitution?

* Is corroboration in the sense required in *R v Baskerville* required in respect of the testimony of accomplice witnesses who have participated in a State Witness Protection Programme? If not, what is the appropriate test in relation to such witnesses?

Held: As the benefits to witnesses under the Witness Protection Programme were perhaps more perceived than real, there was no need to formulate special rules for accomplice witnesses in the Witness Protection Programme. The testimony from persons receiving a benefit under a witness protection programme should be viewed with caution, and while such evidence was not inadmissible, it should be scrutinised carefully. The credibility of such a witness, and the weight of his evidence, should be analysed in the light of all the evidence in the case. However, once a warning was given, the jury could determine the appropriate weight to be attached to such evidence and were entitled to convict in the absence of corroborative evidence. *The People (at the suit of the Director of Public Prosecution) v John Gilligan* [2005] I.E.S.C. 78.

5. Identification Evidence

There are many reasons why eyewitness evidence might be faulty. There are environmental factors like bad weather or poor light leading to bad visibility; physical factors like poor eyesight; cognitive factors like bad memory; and the difficulty that anybody has in remembering a stranger.

Finally, and perhaps most significantly, is the difficulty in testing such evidence. Cross-examination is largely ineffective if a witness is adamant that they saw something, as it is difficult to propose a contrary view.

For these reasons, the testimony of an eyewitness is treated with caution. It is important to note, however, that identification evidence is not necessarily corroborating evidence, but is rather supporting evidence, which is a far broader concept, and not subject to the same strict *Baskerville* requirements.

Key Principle: The trial judge must give a special warning to the jury in any case that depends largely on visual identification evidence.

Attorney-General v Casey (No.2) [1963]

Dominic Casey was convicted of offences for subduing and indecently assaulting two five-year-old boys in a field.

Ann Snailes gave evidence that she had walked with Casey and left him on the road near the field. She remembered that there were children playing in the field, including the two victims of the attack. She had arranged with Casey that he would wait for her there, as she was to be gone for only a few minutes. When she left him, he was wearing an oatmeal-coloured overcoat. When she returned 10 minutes later, Casey was gone.

The critical evidence against Casey was provided by two eyewitnesses. John Mooney, a 12-year-old boy, testified that he had seen Casey walking with the two boys in a field where the attack later took place, and that Casey was wearing a near-white overcoat at the time. Mooney had subsequently pointed Casey out at an identification parade and in the court during the trial.

The second witness, Richard Nohl, gave evidence that he was in his house and had heard a commotion in the field behind his

51

house. He ran out to the field, where he saw the two boys under a tree. Darkness had fallen, but he saw a man running away. Nohl gave chase, but he did not succeed in catching the running person, who was not wearing an overcoat. In the short time that Nohl was with the boys, he did not notice an overcoat and no overcoat was ever found in the vicinity. Nohl ran back to his house and immediately jumped into his car to give chase. He drove down the side road to the convent gates, where he saw a man climbing over the gates. Nohl rammed the gates with his car, causing the man to fall off the gates within the grounds. The man was on the ground in a sitting position, half-facing Nohl. Nohl testified that he saw the man's face for a moment in the headlights of the car and at a distance of about four yards. The glass of one of the car's headlights was smashed in the collision. The man behind the gates ran away.

Nohl identified Casey at an identification parade (where he wore a light-coloured overcoat) and again in court. At the identification parade, Nohl stated that he was not "one-hundred percent sure" as the man on the gate was wearing a blue jacket. At the retrial, Nohl stated that he was at first unwilling to make a positive identification as he was afraid of the attendant publicity.

One of the victims of the attack, James Handyside, did not identify Casey at an identification parade.

Diana Carroll, a young girl, gave unsworn testimony that she had seen the two boys in the field and had seen Casey standing in that field near the wall which formed its boundary.

Casey was convicted in a retrial held in the Central Criminal Court and sentenced to an effective four years' imprisonment.

On appeal, the Court of Criminal Appeal confirmed the conviction, but allowed an appeal to the Supreme Court on a point of law of public importance.

Held: The Supreme Court held that where the verdict depends substantially on the correctness of a visual identification of the accused by an eyewitness, the jury must be warned that in a number of cases visual identification has subsequently been found to be wrong. The direction to the jury should include the statement that it has often been the case that honest witnesses with good observation opportunities have made incorrect identifications, that it is important to examine the identification evidence against the prevailing circumstances and in the light of all of the evidence, that there is a need for special caution, and that the jury must be satisfied beyond all reasonable doubt of the correctness of the identification. Finally, the warning should not be a stereotyped formula, but must be based on the facts of the case. Where the dangers of wrong identification are more apparent, the warning should be stronger. The Supreme Court allowed the appeal and ordered a new trial. *The People (at the suit of the Attorney-General) v Dominic Casey (No.2)(1)* [1963] I.R. 33.

R. v Turnbull [1977]

Raymond Turnbull and Joseph Camelo were convicted of conspiracy to burgle. The evidence was that the night safe of the local bank was put out of action with a bent nail, and thereafter a fraudulent notice was placed over the night safe, instructing users to deposit their takings through the postbox flap. Another notice was placed over the postbox, identifying it as the night safe.

The prosecution alleged that Turnbull and Camelo thereafter planned to break into the bank through a back window and retrieve the monies that had been placed in the unsecured letter-box. A client became suspicious and alerted the police, who lay in wait with the bank manager and his assistant for the culprits to show up. When they heard the notice being removed from the front of the postbox, they ran out.

Testimony was given by the assistant bank manager that he saw a man walking close to the wall near the night safe. He described the man as being five feet eight inches tall, with dark hair and wearing a coat similar to the one that Turnbull was wearing that night. The witness did not see the man's face.

The bank manager gave evidence that he had gone around the front of the bank and noticed a van in the side road next to the bank. He took the registration number. It was common cause that the van had been hired by Camelo and that he was driving it that night. The manager was not able to see the driver of the van. However, one of the police constables testified that he had seen Camelo driving the van slowly past the front of the bank.

The principal identification witness was a Detective Constable Smith. He testified that he saw a man remove a notice from the door of the bank and thereafter remove another notice above the night safe. Smith testified that the man had turned his head and he had recognised the man as Turnbull.

Another witness, Woman Police Constable Thompson, gave evidence that she was on duty in a police vehicle and saw a blue van with two people in it driving at high speed about five minutes after the incident at the bank. They had received a wireless message about the bank incident and gave chase and finally stopped the van. Constable Thompson saw Turnbull stepping onto the pavement from the side of some bushes nearby. Camelo was in the driver's seat. Thompson testified that she went across and searched the bushes and found a number of housebreaking implements.

At the time of their arrest, Turnbull claimed not to know Camelo but it was later admitted by the defence that they did know each other.

The trial judge did warn the jury about the dangers of visual identification. The prosecution argued that although Detective Constable Smith had but a fleeting glimpse of Turnbull, he knew him, and therefore his sighting was a case of recognition rather than identification. In addition, the other evidence supported his evidence.

Held: The court set out some important guidelines for dealing with visual identification evidence:

* where the prosecution's case depends substantially or entirely on visual identification evidence, the trial judge must warn the jury of a special need for caution before convicting on that evidence, and why there is a need for such caution;

* the trial judge must warn the jury to examine the circumstances of the visual identification, for example, the conditions and the extent and duration of the visual identification;

* if the quality of the evidence is good, then the above warning is sufficient, and the jury should be left to consider the evidence. However, if the quality of the evidence is poor, the judge should direct an acquittal, unless there is other evidence which supports the correctness of the identification.

In this case, the Court of Appeal held that once the jury had accepted the honesty of the testimony of Detective Constable Smith, the accuracy of his identification was confirmed by all the other evidence of all the other witnesses. The appeal was refused and the convictions of Turnbull and Camelo were confirmed. *R. v Raymond Turnbull and Joseph Nicholas David Camelo* [1977] 1 Q.B. 224.

Key Principle: Where a witness knows the person they identify, this is strictly recognition evidence as opposed to identification evidence. However, the trial judge should issue the same warning to the jury.

DPP v Stafford [1983]

James Stafford was convicted by a jury of shooting with intent to resist arrest and was sentenced to eight years' imprisonment. The conviction rested primarily on the evidence of a policeman who had previously known Stafford, and who identified him as the person present at the time and place of the offence. As the policeman already knew Stafford, the judge decided that he did not need to give the jury the standard warning about identification evidence, as this was a case of recognition rather than identification.

Held: The Court of Criminal Appeal held that the failure of the judge to give the jury the standard warning of the dangers involved in visual identification rendered his charge to the jury a misdirection.

The court set aside the verdict and ordered a retrial. *The People (at the suit of the Director of Public Prosecutions) v James Stafford* [1983] I.R. 165.

Commentary
A similar finding was made by the Court of Criminal Appeal in its decision of *DPP v David Smith* [1999] 2 I.L.R.M. 161.

Key Principle: It is prejudicial to the accused if a witness is permitted to identify him for the first time in court (a "dock identification"), as the witness may feel pressurised by the circumstances of the courtroom and the trial to make a positive identification. Although these dock identifications are not inadmissible per se, the weight to be attached to them must be limited.

DPP v Cooney [1998]

Christopher Cooney was charged with murder. At his trial, the evidence of a first and second identification parade was held inadmissible. The trial judge did, however, allow a dock identification, despite the objections of the defence. The jury convicted Cooney.

Held: The Supreme Court held that the criminal law had for a long time recognised that dock identifications were undesirable and unsatisfactory. The identification of the accused when he or she is sitting in the place reserved for the accused and flanked by prison officers is of little probative value. The appropriate procedure is to hold an identification parade before the trial, where the identification of the accused is likely to be an issue.

In the present case, however, the trial judge was aware that identification parades had taken place but the evidence of those were subsequently disallowed, not because of any fault in the identification parade, but because of questions concerning the legality of Cooney's continued detention. The judge had not only warned the jury about the dangers of identification evidence, but had specifically warned the jury about the dangers of dock identification. The trial judge was entitled to use his discretion and allow the evidence of the dock identification in court, as long as he was of the view that its probative value outweighed its prejudicial nature. *The People (at the suit of the Director of Public Prosecutions) v Christopher Cooney* [1998] 1 I.L.R.M. 321.

Commentary
The ideal situation is that the accused is identified at an identification parade and this identification is confirmed during the trial. This practice has been commended by the Court of Criminal Appeal in the decisions of *DPP v O'Reilly* [1995] 2 I.R. 415 and *DPP v Duff* [1995] 3 I.R. 296, despite earlier decisions of the Supreme Court holding that there was no hard and fast rule concerning identification parades and that each case must be considered on its own facts. *People (A-G) v Martin* [1956] I.R. 22; *People (A-G) v Fagan* (1974) 1 Frewen 375.

Key Principle: In instances where the accused refuses to take part in a formal identification parade, an informal identification may be carried out, but the procedure used must be fair to the accused.

DPP v Rapple [1999]

The victim of a robbery gave a description of his attacker that included the detail that the robber had a tattoo of a bird between his thumb and forefinger. The victim thereafter identified Michael Rapple amongst a series of photographs.

Rapple was arrested and charged, but refused to take part in an identification parade. He was released pending trial. The victim was taken in a car and identified Rapple walking down the road.

Rapple objected to this form of identification.

Held: The Court of Criminal Appeal held that the use of photographs to arrive at a suspect is fair, provided that the suspect is thereafter identified in the flesh. This should be done by means of a formal identification parade. However, if the suspect refuses a formal identification parade, then the Gardaí must seek to create a situation where a personal identification can be made of the suspect in conditions of fairness. What the Gardaí did in the present case was reasonable and fair.

The court went on to say that there are two separate and distinct situations where photographs might be shown to a witness. There is the situation where photographs are shown to a complainant in an effort to find a suspect. There is the other situation where the accused is already in custody and an identification parade is due to be held but before the parade the complainant is shown photographs from which the accused can be identified. The second situation is clearly unfair and prejudicial to the accused. The facts of the present case fell squarely in the first situation and, as such, the court had no objection to the use of photographs in these circumstances. *The People (at the suit of the Director of Public Prosecutions) v Michael Rapple* [1999] 1 I.L.R.M. 113.

Key Principle: Video evidence, like photographs, is admissible to identify the accused.

DPP v Maguire [1995]

Thomas Maguire was convicted of robbing a building society where the primary evidence was footage from a security camera.

Maguire appealed his conviction on the ground that the trial judge had failed to adequately direct the jury as to the manner in which visual identification evidence from a video might be used.

Held: The Court of Criminal Appeal held that although the evidence of the video film was admissible, the usual and proper warning required in relation to identification evidence must be given to the jury. This warning must include the principle that a jury should only seek to form its own view as to the identity of the accused where there is no independent evidence of identification; and in those circumstances a jury may use such view together with its view of the other evidence led in court in reaching a decision. In doing so, a member of the jury is not to be regarded as acting as an expert, but is doing no more than a person in typical domestic, social or other situations does from time to time, namely, identifying a person in a photograph as a person he is then looking at or whom he has recently seen. *The People (at the suit of the Director of Public Prosecutions) v Thomas Maguire* [1995] 2 I.R. 286.

Commentary

The English Court of Appeal reached a similar decision on almost identical facts in its decision of *R. v Dodson; R. v Williams* [1984] 1 W.L.R. 971. The factual difference in this case was that the three armed robbers ran away empty-handed, and later confessed to the robbery when apprehended, with Williams commenting on the pictures taken by the security camera: "I heard the photos were good but not that good".

Despite this, an appeal was made against the trial judge's ruling that pictures taken by a security camera were admissible as evidence. The Court of Appeal rejected this argument and confirmed that photographs taken at the scene of a crime are highly relevant and accordingly admissible. The Court of Appeal confirmed that the trial judge had to give the usual warning about the dangers of identification evidence, and thereafter it was up to the jury to decide on the weight of the photographic evidence.

6. Evidence about Similar Criminal Conduct

If an accused has previous convictions, it is recognised that it might be dangerous for the jury to be told of these, as they might close their minds and prejudge the accused, along the lines of "a leopard does not change his spots".

This type of evidence is often described under the heading "similar fact evidence", which is a title that has survived from the common law and a time when the prosecution was allowed to lead evidence of the previous crimes of the accused, as long as the crime that was currently before the court was similar to those previous crimes. Although courts now try to avoid using the phrase, the essential logic behind that rule remains.

There are two methods by which prosecuting counsel might try and get this evidence into court "underneath the radar". First, they might ask a witness during examination-in-chief about the accused's past. Secondly, the accused might be asked about his past whilst under cross-examination. The manner in which the law deals with these situations is different and, therefore, this chapter will deal with the first aspect—the question of this evidence being led during examination-in-chief—and the next chapter will deal with the second aspect—questions being asked of the accused during cross-examination.

The current test is similar to the general test of admissibility—what has to be decided is whether the prejudice created by such evidence is outweighed by its probative value—in other words, its usefulness in determining the issues before the court. It is not always enough that evidence of previous conduct is *similar* to the evidence being considered under the current charges; rather, evidence of prior conduct should help to determine whether the accused committed the present conduct.

Key Principle: The evidence of a previous crime may be admissible if it is sufficiently relevant to the extent that it tends to show whether the deeds of the accused were accidental or by design, or whether the evidence might rebut a defence which is available to the accused.

Makin v Attorney-General for New South Wales **[1894]**

John Makin and Sarah Makin, a husband and wife, were charged with the murder of their adopted baby.

Evidence was led that after discussions between the Makins and the mother of the child, the child was handed over to them with a view to adoption. A sum of money was also paid to the Makins, sufficient to support the child for a limited period. The child's remains were discovered in the garden of a house previously occupied by the Makins. Further investigation revealed that the bodies of other children were buried in the gardens of three houses that the Makins had previously occupied. Four bodies were discovered at George Street, six bodies were discovered at the couple's present house at Burren Street, along with the body of the baby for which they were presently charged, and the bones of two decomposed bodies were discovered at a house the couple had first occupied at Levy Street.

The evidence was that the Makins had struck similar deals with other mothers who had handed over their children in similar circumstances, namely, that the couple was supposed to adopt the child, and had been given sums of money adequate to support the child for a limited period during the process of adoption.

In other words, the prosecution wanted to show that the couple were killing the children and keeping the money for themselves. The prosecution also wanted to lead the evidence of these other bodies, but the defence objected, as this was evidence of previous criminal conduct.

Held: The Privy Council found that, as a general rule, it is not permitted to lead evidence showing that the accused has been guilty of criminal acts not covered by the present indictment solely for the purpose of inferring that the accused is likely to have committed the offence currently under consideration.

On the other hand, if the evidence is relevant to the issues currently before the court, and if that relevance is based on the fact that it could answer the question whether the illegal acts were purposely done or by accident, or to rebut a defence which would otherwise be available to the accused, it could be admissible.

On the facts before the court, the evidence was admissible to rebut the defence of inevitable accident. *John Makin and Sarah Makin, his Wife, v The Attorney-General for New South Wales* [1894] A.C. 57.

Commentary
The decision in *Makin* was a victory for common sense, as clearly the evidence was extremely relevant to the issues.

Whether it meant that the accused couple had murdered the baby in question can be debated, and that is one of the criticisms of this "similar-fact" evidence, as critics argue that the jury will find a person guilty in order to punish the accused for his previous crimes, as opposed to the crime with which the accused is currently charged. Some would not have a problem with this, as it could be called just rewards, but that cannot be a justification from an evidential point of view.

The other obvious problem with the judgment in *Makin* is that the Privy Council did not lay down any guidelines or principles to help a court decide whether the evidence under consideration does answer the question of whether the actions of the accused were deliberate or accidental or whether it could be used to rebut a defence.

Despite these problems, the decision has been followed in Ireland.

Attorney-General v Kirwan [1943]

Bernard Kirwan was convicted of the murder of his brother, Laurence Kirwan. Bernard and Laurence had lived together on the family farm, near Tullamore in County Offaly.

The corpse of the victim had been discovered in a nearby bog. The arms, legs, pelvis, and head were missing, the body having been dismembered, apparently by blows from a chopper or hatchet.

The prosecution sought to lead evidence that whilst Bernard Kirwan was in prison for another offence, he had been trained as a butcher, which would have meant that he had the expertise to sever the limbs from the torso of his brother.

The evidence of experts established that the dismemberment of the body could have properly been done only by a person possessed of some anatomical skill and knowledge, such as a doctor, a veterinary surgeon, or a butcher. The evidence of John Kelleher was led by the prosecution to show that Bernard Kirwan had that skill and knowledge. Kelleher testified that, on several occasions, Bernard Kirwan had performed "operations" on the carcases of pigs, and these operations were very similar to, if not identical with, the operations that had been performed on the torso of Laurence Kirwan.

The other evidence that was linked to the accused's prison sentence was that at the time of his disappearance, Laurence Kirwan was carrying a considerable sum of money—possibly £200—and that after Laurence disappeared, Bernard was spending money freely and had in his possession more than £80. The prosecution suggested that the money found on Bernard was Laurence's money and that it could not have been money earned and saved by Bernard, who had not been in a position to earn anything for several years, as he had been in jail. This was established by the evidence of Mr Burrows, and his testimony was that Bernard did not earn anything between the year 1937 and the month of June, 1941, and that on his discharge from prison in that month the only money that he had was £2 11s. 8d.

Despite the objections of the defence, the trial judge allowed this evidence to be led.

Bernard Kirwan applied to the Court of Criminal Appeal for leave to appeal against his conviction. One of the grounds of his appeal was that the trial judge was wrong in law in admitting evidence which disclosed to the jury that he had previously been convicted of a criminal offence. The Court of Criminal Appeal refused the application for leave to appeal, but issued a certificate allowing Bernard Kirwan to appeal their decision to the Supreme Court.

One of the questions before the Supreme Court was whether evidence which disclosed that the accused had served a term of penal servitude for another offence was admissible at the trial.

Held: The Supreme Court held that evidence which disclosed that the accused had committed an offence other than that charged in the indictment was admissible as being relevant to an issue which the jury had to determine.

The Supreme Court was at pains to point out that the offence for which the accused had been previously imprisoned was never mentioned and that, in addition, the trial judge had been emphatic in his directions to the jury that the fact of the accused's previous imprisonment should not be used against him, or against his character, or as rendering it likely, or tending to show, that he committed the murder, or to prejudice him in any way in his defence in the current trial. The evidence was admissible in determining whether the accused had committed the murder for which he was being charged. *The People (at the suit of the Attorney-General) v Bernard Kirwan* [1943] I.R. 279.

Key Principle: In order for evidence of previous misconduct of the accused to be admissible, the previous misconduct must show a systematic course of conduct by the accused or must be strikingly similar to the conduct which is the subject of the charges currently under consideration.

Boardman v DPP [1974]

Derrick Boardman, a headmaster, was charged under three counts, namely buggery with S; inciting H to commit buggery, and inciting A to commit buggery. He was convicted of attempted buggery under count 1, and was convicted under counts 2 and 3.

One of Boardman's grounds of appeal was that the judge had erred in directing the jury that the evidence on count 2 was capable of amounting to corroboration on count 1 and vice versa, as the defence raised was not a specific defence which could be rebutted by similar fact evidence (following *Makin*), but was rather a defence of general denial, as Boardman denied that the alleged incidents had happened at all.

Boardman also argued that the judge had erred in law by directing the jury that because the type of behaviour alleged in each of counts 1 and 2 was of a particular or unusual kind, the evidence of such behaviour under each separate count was mutually corroborative.

Held: The House of Lords refused the appeal and confirmed the conviction. The Lords held that where the criminal acts on the part of the accused (other than those with which he was charged) bore a striking similarity to other acts being investigated and where those acts were of probative force, the evidence about those strikingly similar criminal acts might be admissible. It was for the trial judge to decide whether the prejudice to the accused was outweighed by the probative force of the evidence and to rule accordingly.

On the facts of the present case, the trial judge had been entitled to direct the jury as he had done. *Derrick Rowland Boardman v the Director for Public Prosecutions* [1975] A.C. 421.

Commentary

Although the theory behind the "systematic course of conduct" and "strikingly similar" tests is sound, the practice of deciding whether these tests are applicable can be time-consuming and open to interpretation by the trial judge. Time-consuming because the trial judge will need to go through a lot of evidence to decide whether there are striking similarities, and open to interpretation because it is not clear what type of evidence should be considered—evidence of previous convictions is one thing, but evidence of previous misconduct is another. Who is to say that the defendant was guilty of misconduct? Is it enough that he was previously charged with misconduct or should he be convicted of the conduct before evidence of it can be led?

The House of Lords recognised that the concept of striking similarity was open to interpretation and purposely left the concept open-ended, rather than defining it. What this means, in practice, is that whilst one trial judge might decide that evidence is strikingly similar, another trial judge might look at that same evidence and disagree that there are striking similarities. A good example of this is the contrasting decisions of *Novak* and *Johannsen*.

R. v Novak (1977)

Andrew Novak was charged with acts of procuring and committing acts of sexual indecency with other males.

The evidence led by the prosecution firstly consisted of the testimony of various police officers who had observed Novak in and around an amusement arcade near Piccadilly Circus called *Playland*, which was a popular meeting point for young male prostitutes and their customers.

The second lot of evidence came from youths of various ages under 21 years who testified about indecent acts committed between themselves and Novak, mostly at his house.

The third lot of evidence was a series of written statements made by Novak containing damaging admissions.

The question before the court was to what extent the evidence led in relation to the conspiracy and related counts was admissible as being relevant to, and capable of, providing corroboration of the evidence of the young boys concerned in the specific offence counts.

Held: The Court of Appeal held that the question was ultimately one for the exercise of the trial judge's discretion. But, if in a homosexual case, one group of offences is not connected with another by features of such striking similarity as would make the evidence mutually relevant and corroborative, the considerations mentioned by Lord Cross of Chelsea in *Boardman* must, at least in the vast majority of cases, be decisive as to how the discretion should be exercised.

The court relied on the judgment of Lord Salmon in *Boardman* where he said that evidence which proves merely that the accused has committed crimes in the past, and is, therefore, disposed to commit the crime charged, is clearly inadmissible. Lord Salmon continued to say that it has, however, never been doubted that if the crime charged is committed in a uniquely, or strikingly, similar manner to other crimes committed by the accused, the manner in which the other crimes were committed may be evidence upon which a jury could reasonably conclude that the accused was guilty of the crime charged. The similarity would have to be so unique or striking that common sense makes it inexplicable on the basis of coincidence.

The court quashed three of Novak's convictions but confirmed the sentence and refused him leave to appeal to the House of Lords. *R. v Andrew Novak* (1977) 65 Cr.App.R. 107.

R. v Johannsen (1977)

Vincent Johannsen was charged with buggery and gross indecency on five schoolboys aged between 14 and 15. The defence sought to have separate trials in respect of each complainant. The trial judge ruled against the motion on the ground that the evidence of the complainants' written depositions revealed striking similarities between the separate counts. Johannsen was convicted and sentenced to concurrent terms of life imprisonment on the buggery counts and to five years' imprisonment concurrent on each of the gross indecency counts.

Johannsen appealed and one of the grounds of appeal was that the evidence had revealed that four of the boys knew each other, two of them being close friends, and he argued that the trial judge should have inferred that there was a real chance that the boys could have concocted the story between them. On that basis, the indictment should have been severed and separate trials held.

Held: The Court of Appeal held that there were striking similarities about what happened to the boys: they were all accosted in the same kind of place (an amusement arcade); the same method of enticement was used (offering money or a meal); there were similarities in the evidence from the boys concerning the accused's propensities and his ways of gratifying them; and Johannsen had made oral statements and a written statement admitting to gross indecency with one of the boys, which was corroboration of that boy's evidence. In many cases of sexual assault it was likely that the victims would know each other. This was not a reason, on its own, to reject their evidence. That was up to the jury when they decided on the weight of the evidence, and all the trial judge should do is to remind the jury to consider whether there has been collusion and concoction between the victims. In this case, the trial judge had so instructed the jury.

The conviction was confirmed but the concurrent life sentences were reduced to seven years' imprisonment on each count of buggery, to run concurrently. *R. v Vincent Paul Johannsen* (1977) 65 Cr.App.R. 101.

Commentary
Leaving the trial judge with discretion ensures that there will be cases where trial judges reach different conclusions on what seems to be the same evidence in the same circumstances. That is the nature of discretion and unless that discretion is exercised unfairly or capriciously, the appeal court should not interfere.

The problem is larger than that of a trial judge's discretion, however. Types of offences often have similar modes of perpetration—what is called "stock in trade" behaviour. Therefore, for previous criminal conduct to be strikingly similar, that conduct must not be "stock in trade" behaviour usually associated with that crime. Its striking quality must be its unusual features, rather than its usual ones.

Key Principle: The question that needs to be asked in deciding whether to admit evidence on the basis of its striking similarity is whether the probative force of that evidence arising from such similarities is so great as to make it just to admit it, notwithstanding that it is prejudicial to the accused, in that it indicates that he was guilty of another crime.

DPP v P. [1991]

The accused was charged with the rape of, and incest with, both of his daughters. The trial judge refused an application by the defence that the counts relating to each daughter should be heard separately. The accused was convicted of the rape of one daughter, and of incest with both of them.

The accused appealed his conviction on the basis of the refusal of the trial judge to have separate trials, and the Appeal Court upheld his appeal and quashed the conviction. The prosecution appealed this decision to the House of Lords.

Held: The House of Lords held that when deciding whether to admit evidence of previous misconduct on the basis of striking similarities between that conduct and the conduct which was the basis of the current charge, the question in deciding admissibility is whether its probative force is so great as to outweigh the prejudice to the defendant in showing that he was guilty of another crime. Although such probative force might be from the striking similarities in the manner in which the crime was carried out, the principle was not restricted to such cases, and the question of whether the probative value of such evidence outweighed the prejudicial effect to the accused was always one of degree.

The evidence of the daughters established a prolonged course of conduct by the accused towards them, including the use of threats and force, resulting in overall domination, and the fact that he paid for both of them to have abortions.

This evidence, taken together, gave strong probative force to the evidence of the one daughter in respect of the incidents involving the other and was sufficient to justify the admission of such evidence, notwithstanding its prejudicial effect.

The appeal of the prosecution was upheld and the conviction confirmed. *Director of Public Prosecutions v P.* [1991] 2 A.C. 447.

Key Principle: Following English law, the "striking similarities" test has been replaced in Ireland by the "probative force" test.

DPP v B.K. [2000]

The accused was charged with several counts of indecent assault and attempted buggery against various boys. His application to have the trials relating to each complainant separated was refused by the trial judge, and the complainants were heard together. The accused appealed this decision by the trial judge.

Held: The Court of Criminal Appeal held that multiple accusation evidence was allowed in two main types of cases. The first case was where the evidence could establish that the same person committed each offence because of the particular feature common to each. The second case was where the charges were against one person only, and here the evidence could be used to establish that offences were committed by the inherent improbability of several persons making up exactly similar stories.

The test as to whether several counts should be heard together was whether the evidence in each count would be admissible on each of the other counts. To be so admissible, it was necessary that the probative value of such evidence should be greater than its prejudicial effect on the defence of the accused. The rules of evidence should not be allowed to offend common sense.

Applying these principles to the present case, the evidence went no further than saying that because the accused was charged with the offences against one boy, he was more likely to have committed the offences alleged against the other boys. What the trial judge should have been looking for was a series of facts relating to the alleged criminal activity which were such that a jury properly charged, might hold that offences were committed in each case, that they were committed by the same person, and, where necessary to prove a specific intent, that they were committed with the same such intent.

The appeal was upheld and the conviction quashed. Having regard to the time that the accused had already spent in prison, the court did not order a retrial. *The People (at the suit of the Director of Public Prosecutions) v B.K.* [2000] 2 I.R. 199.

Commentary
The "probative value" test should be seen as a refinement, and not a complete replacement, of the "striking similarities" test. The test of striking similarity is unquestionably practical and useful, but what a jury needs to be directed to do is not just to match up the similar facts, but rather to decide if the matched facts go some way to resolving the issue presently before the court—did the accused commit the crime for which he is currently charged?

The trial judge needs to decide whether the jury should ever be allowed to consider this question, or whether the evidence should be kept away from them altogether.

Key Principle: The rules surrounding similar fact evidence do not only apply to the prosecution, they also apply to the defence.

R. v Redgrave (1982)

Scott Redgrave was charged with persistently importuning for an immoral purpose contrary to s.32 of the Sexual Offences Act 1956. The evidence was that five police officers kept plain clothes observation on public toilets in Portsmouth. During that time, Redgrave went in and out of the toilets four times. On two occasions he followed an officer into the toilet. Inside, he masturbated for about a minute near the urinal in the presence of each of the officers who had gone into the toilet separately. The officers testified that Redgrave masturbated openly, noisily and violently and stared at them while doing so. He was taken out of the toilet and cautioned. He told the officers that he had merely been satisfying his lust, because his girlfriend was away. He denied trying to attract other men and said he had felt like masturbating as he passed the public toilets. He said he did not know why he had not gone to his home nearby and did not know why he had not used a cubicle. He agreed that his actions looked bad. He repeated that defence at his trial.

At the trial, Redgrave produced five bundles of documents, which he described as love letters. The documents included photographs of himself with five different girls, all taken in circumstances where the inference would have been that he was on intimate terms with the girls. In the course of his evidence at the first trial, he said that he had been to the home of one of his girlfriends a number of times and he gave the jury the impression, without actually saying so, that he had had sexual intercourse with her.

The defence argued that such evidence was highly probative as it showed that Redgrave was a heterosexual and unlikely to proposition other men. The trial judge refused the application to lead this evidence.

Redgrave was convicted and fined £50 and ordered to pay £100 towards the costs of the prosecution. He appealed his conviction on the ground that the trial judge was wrong in not allowing the evidence to show his sexual disposition.

Held: The Court of Appeal held that the defence was bound by the principles of *Makin* which precluded evidence showing disposition or proclivity. The trial judge's decision was confirmed and the appeal was dismissed. Redgrave was refused leave to appeal to the House of Lords. *R. v Scott Redgrave* (1982) 74 Cr. App. R.10.

Key Principle: The principles surrounding the reception of similar fact evidence also apply in civil trials. However, as very few civil trials now occur before a jury, and are generally before a judge only, these principles are not as rigorously enforced.

Mood Music Publishing v De Wolfe [1976]

The plaintiff and defendant were both music publishers supplying background music for television programmes.

In 1964 the plaintiffs acquired the copyright in a musical work entitled "Sogno Nostalgico" with exclusive rights to use it in the United Kingdom. In 1967 they complained to the defendants that their copyright in "Sogno Nostalgico" had been infringed by the defendants in the making and reproduction of a musical work called "Girl in the Dark". The defendants' reply then, and repeated on a later similar complaint in 1970, was that they had taken an assignment of the copyright in "Girl in the Dark" from its composer in 1966 and that its resemblance to the plaintiffs' work was coincidental.

In December 1970 the plaintiffs issued a writ alleging infringement of their copyright and asking for an injunction and other relief. When the matter came to trial, the plaintiffs still relied on simple infringement but sought to lead evidence of "similar facts" as relevant to the question of whether the similarity of the two works was coincidental or due to copying. This evidence included details of two recordings of two works issued under the defendants' name bearing marked similarity to works of well-known composers which were still in copyright.

The defendants objected to evidence of "similar facts" being introduced into a civil action for infringement of copyright where there was no allegation of fraud or dishonesty. The judge listened to the recordings and thereafter ruled that they were admissible on the issue of coincidence or copying. The defendants appealed this finding.

Held: The Court of Appeal held that evidence of past similar facts may be admitted if it is logically probative, and also if the trial judge is certain that the admission of that evidence is not oppressive or unfair to the other side. The court also pointed out that when it is sought to admit such evidence, the other side must be given adequate notice of this intention so that it has an adequate opportunity to deal with it. *Mood Music Publishing Company Ltd v De Wolfe Ltd* [1976] Ch. 119.

7. Evidence of Previous Convictions and Bad Character Arising during Cross-Examination

If the accused elects to testify in his defence, he is making himself available for cross-examination by the prosecution and by the other accused in a joint trial, and he cannot later argue that this offends his right to silence.

A statutory amendment to the common law by the Criminal Justice (Evidence) Act of 1924 removed the common law prohibition of the accused testifying at his own trial, and similarly specified that the accused could not refuse to answer questions that would tend to incriminate him once he had elected to testify (s.1(e)).

If the accused cannot refuse to be cross-examined, what can the accused be asked during cross-examination and, more specifically, can he be asked about previous convictions and evidence of bad character? If these questions are allowed during cross-examination, would that not discourage the accused from testifying in his own defence, even in cases where it might show his innocence? On the other hand, if these questions were disallowed during cross-examination, this would give the accused free licence to describe himself in glowing terms, knowing that this could not be contradicted.

Section 1(f) of the 1924 Act attempts to provide a compromise between these two conflicting positions, by saying that such questions can be asked in three situations. First, they can be asked if such evidence was admissible to show that the accused committed the offence currently under consideration. This is similar to the principle laid down in the previous chapter, and is essentially a question of balancing the probative value versus the prejudicial value of the evidence in deciding its admissibility. Secondly, these questions can be asked if the accused "opens the door" to character evidence by testifying about his or her own good character, or questioning the prosecution witnesses as to their character. Finally, such questions are permissible if the accused gives evidence as an accomplice witness against another accused in another trial.

Obviously s.1(f) only comes into operation once the accused decides to testify at his own trial. If he maintains his silence, the section has no part to play.

Key Principle: Evidence led under the first exception mentioned in s.1(f) can only be used to prove the guilt of the accused, whereas evidence led under the other two exceptions can only be used to assess the credibility of the accused.

Attorney-General v Bond [1966]

Denis Bond was charged with stopping a post office van with intent to rob the van. His counsel asked many questions of the prosecution witnesses which the trial judge accepted as being such as to "involve imputations on the character" of such witnesses. As a result, the trial judge allowed Bond to be cross-examined on his previous convictions, which included a conviction for the violent robbery of a wages van.

The jury convicted Bond, and he appealed his conviction.

Held: The Court of Criminal Appeal held that although the trial judge could not be faulted for allowing the cross-examination of Bond about his previous convictions, he should have directed the jury that this evidence was before the jury for one purpose only, namely, to consider whether Bond was a person whose own testimony might not be believed. It could not be used to suggest that it was likely that Bond had committed the robbery in question on the basis of what he had done before.

The appeal was upheld and a retrial ordered. *The People (at the suit of the Attorney-General) v Denis G. H. Bond* (1) [1966] I.R. 214.

Commentary

Although this distinction is an important one, it is very difficult to enforce in practice, because one cannot really control what the jury makes of evidence once it has it in mind. In other words, once the accused has been discredited in the eyes of the jury, that same jury will be easily convinced that the accused has committed the crime in question. Accordingly, the distinction between credibility and issue is collapsed. As a matter of practice, however, the trial judge should instruct the jury correctly on the use of the evidence obtained from the accused under cross-examination. Whether or not the jury will listen to the trial judge is another matter altogether.

Key Principle: Evidence of previous convictions or bad character is inadmissible if it reveals for the first time during cross-examination that the accused has a previous conviction for a similar offence.

Jones v DPP [1962]

Albert Jones was convicted of murder on June 19, 1961. The victim was a young girl who had not returned home from a Girl Guide meeting on October 28, 1960. When her body was found, it appeared that she had been indecently assaulted and strangled. Some three months before his trial for murder, Jones had been convicted for the rape of another young girl. The victim had been attacked on her way home from a Girl Guide meeting in September 1960. There were significant similarities between the two cases.

During the second trial (for murder), as a result of the cross-examination of a police officer by Jones's counsel and also his own evidence-in-chief, the jury was aware that Jones had earlier had "trouble with the police". The trial judge allowed the prosecution to cross-examine Jones about these previous incidents as he had used an alibi during his defence of the rape charge and it seemed he had now changed his alibi when charged with this murder.

Jones was convicted and sentenced to life imprisonment. He appealed his conviction, claiming that the trial judge had contravened s.1(f) of the Criminal Evidence Act of 1898 (the English equivalent of s.1(f) of the 1924 Act in Ireland) by allowing questions about his previous conviction during his cross-examination. The Court of Appeal confirmed the conviction and the matter went to the House of Lords.

Held: The House of Lords ruled that the prohibition contained in the statute only came into play when the evidence of previous convictions or bad character was revealed for the first time during cross-examination. In this case, the jury was well aware of Jones's character as a result of earlier evidence, and therefore the prohibition did not apply. The appeal was refused, and the life sentence confirmed. *Albert Arthur Jones v the Director of Public Prosecutions* [1962] A.C. 635.

Commentary
This is what is meant by "opening the door". If it is the accused who first raises the issue of character, he or she cannot later complain that the prosecution has pursued the issue of character when the time comes for his or her cross-examination.

Key Principle: Section 1(f) would not prohibit evidence of a previous acquittal of the accused if that evidence was relevant to the issue of the accused's character.

Maxwell v DPP [1935]

William Maxwell was a doctor charged with manslaughter, the prosecution leading evidence that he had caused the death of a young woman whilst committing an illegal abortion upon her. During his evidence, Maxwell testified about his good character and, as a result, the prosecution was allowed to cross-examine him about the fact that he had previously been charged with manslaughter, under similar circumstances, although he had been acquitted of that charge.

Maxwell was convicted but appealed on the basis that evidence of his previous charge and acquittal should never have been allowed into the court.

Held: The Court of Appeal agreed with Maxwell, and quashed his conviction. The court said that in order for evidence of a previous charge and acquittal to be relevant, it had to be relevant to the issue of the accused's character, or relevant to an issue before the jury. This evidence did not qualify as either because the evidence of the previous charge did not impair the credibility of Maxwell as a witness, as the fact that a person was charged did not mean that he had committed the offence, and the evidence of the acquittal was not relevant to the issues before the jury for the same reason.

The Court of Appeal held further that if such evidence was allowed it could lead the minds of the jury astray and would detract from the issue before the jury, namely did Maxwell commit the crime currently before the court? However, this was not the same as saying that there is a complete prohibition against questions showing that a person was charged but acquitted of a similar offence. Such questions might be relevant to an issue before the jury, for example, whether the accused was angry at the complainant who had made the complaint leading to the charge for which he was acquitted. *William Maxwell v The Director of Public Prosecutions* [1935] A.C. 309.

Commentary
This confirms the overriding consideration when assessing the admissibility of character evidence: does its probative value outweigh its prejudicial effect? If not, it cannot be allowed.

Key Principle: If the accused gives evidence as to his good character, he can be cross-examined on his character. In contrast, if character witnesses are called on behalf of the accused, this does not "open the door" to allow cross-examination on his character; the prosecution would need to call their own character witnesses in rebuttal.

DPP v Ferris [2002]

William Ferris was convicted on 32 counts of indecent assault on a male person contrary to s.62 of the Offences against the Person Act 1861. The offences were charged as having been committed over a period of nine years, from 1983 to 1992, against a person who was only four years of age at the beginning of the period and thirteen years of age at the end.

During the trial, Ferris's two aunts gave evidence on his behalf. The first aunt, who had two children, a boy and a girl, was asked about contact between Ferris and her own children, and she testified that he would often take the children out and that the children had never made any complaints about him. The second aunt had two girls and she testified that the two girls had often been alone with Ferris and neither child had raised any complaint. The second aunt continued to say that she thought the allegations against Ferris were untrue.

The prosecution argued that this evidence constituted evidence as to the character of Ferris, thereby allowing cross-examination on his character and previous conduct. The trial judge agreed and the prosecution thereafter forced Ferris to admit that paedophile pornography had been found in his flat.

Held: The Court of Criminal Appeal held that the only evidence which was permitted at a criminal trial was evidence that was relevant as to whether the accused had committed the act in question. The Criminal Justice (Evidence) Act 1924 provided that in certain circumstances an accused could be cross-examined as to his character. These circumstances were based on the accused himself giving evidence as to his character. Section 1(f) did not apply when a witness other than the accused gave character evidence. The common law prevailed in this matter and the law was that when the defence called character witnesses, the prosecution was allowed to call character witnesses in rebuttal. In

this instance, the protection afforded to Ferris under the 1924 Act
had not been lost and the trial judge had wrongly permitted Ferris
to be cross-examined as to his character. *The People (at the suit
of the Director of Public Prosecutions) v William Ferris,*
unreported, June 10, 2002.

Key Principle: The accused may make imputations against the
character of a prosecution witness without exposing himself to bad
character cross-examination where the imputations were reasonably
necessary to enable him to establish his defence.

DPP v McGrail [1990]

John McGrail was charged with various offences under the Firearms
Act of 1945. The prosecution's case was that he had made a number
of incriminating statements to the Gardaí, and, amongst other things,
had told them the location of hidden firearms, but he had refused to
sign a written statement.

During the trial, defence counsel put it to the Garda witnesses
that McGrail did not make any incriminating statements and that
these had been concocted by the investigating officer.

The trial judge allowed cross-examination on bad character and
previous convictions, and McGrail was forced to admit that he had
been convicted seven times for the theft of motor cars and once for
possessing housebreaking implements (subsequently overturned on
appeal).

Not surprisingly, McGrail was convicted of the firearms offences
and he appealed on the grounds that the trial judge had wrongfully
allowed cross-examination on his previous offences.

Held: The Court of Criminal Appeal upheld the appeal and
quashed the conviction. The Court pointed out that the only defence
available to McGrail was to question the evidence of the
incriminating statements, as the prosecution's case rested upon
these.

The court said a distinction had to be drawn between questions
which are reasonably necessary to establish a case or a defence,
and questions imputing bad character relating to matters unconnected
with the issues before the jury or the evidence of the case. The
court held that a procedure which inhibits the accused from
challenging the veracity of the evidence against him because of the

threat of his own character being put in evidence cannot be said to be a fair procedure. *The People (at the suit of the Director of Public Prosecutions) v John McGrail* [1990] 2 I.R. 38.

Commentary
The approach by the Court of Criminal Appeal in *McGrail* is much stricter (and fairer to the accused) than the wide approach adopted by the House of Lords (*Selvey v DPP* [1970] A.C. 304) and indeed, perhaps even by our own Supreme Court (*AG v Campbell* [1945] I.R. 237). The logic and fairness of Hederman J. cannot be faulted, and his purposive approach is to be preferred to the literal approach adopted by the House of Lords, which, it must be argued, could be seen as imposing undue restrictions on the right of the accused to mount a full defence.

Key Principle: The accused can be examined regarding both character and previous convictions where he has testified against a co-accused.

Murdoch v Taylor [1965]

Adam Murdoch, "with a record of criminal offences", was charged with another accused, Neil John Lynch, for receiving cameras knowing that they were stolen. Murdoch had testified that he did not know what was in the box, that the box was with Lynch, and that he was oblivious of the transaction which had been performed by Lynch. The trial judge held that counsel for Lynch was entitled to cross-examine Murdoch regarding his character and previous convictions.

Both men were convicted and Murdoch appealed his conviction, arguing that the trial judge was wrong in allowing such cross-examination.

Held: The House of Lords confirmed the conviction. The court held that the phrase "evidence against" means evidence which supports the prosecution's case in a material respect or undermines the defence of the co-accused and it is not necessary that the witness should have a hostile intent against his co-accused. What is said in cross-examination is just as much a part of the witness's evidence as what is said in examination-in-chief.

The court continued by holding that once the trial judge had ruled that the witness has given evidence against his co-accused, that trial judge must allow cross-examination on his previous convictions—he had no discretion to disallow such cross-examination. The court recognised that this was in contrast to the treatment given to the other two statutory exceptions in the paragraph, but held that the distinction was justified as a co-accused has a right to defend himself against conviction and this right of defence must not be fettered in any way. *Adam Murdoch v James Taylor (Police Constable)* [1965] A.C. 574.

R. v Varley (1982)

Joseph Varley, along with a co-accused named Dibble, was charged with armed robbery after a post office raid had been carried out by a man armed with a sawn-off shotgun. Varley had been on weekend leave from prison at the time of the robbery, and had already served two lengthy prison sentences for armed robbery.

Dibble admitted to participating in the robbery with Varley, but claimed that he had done so only because Varley had threatened his life. Varley denied the evidence of Dibble, claiming that he was lying.

The question before the trial judge was whether this denial was evidence "against" his co-accused, Dibble, which would allow Dibble's counsel to cross-examine Varley about his previous convictions for armed robbery. The trial judge allowed Varley to be cross-examined on his previous convictions.

Both Varley and Dibble were convicted of armed robbery. Varley appealed his conviction, with one of his grounds of appeal being that the trial judge was wrong in allowing Dibble's counsel to cross-examine him about his previous convictions as his denial was not evidence against Dibble.

Held: The Court of Appeal laid down the following guidelines:

- that the term "evidence against" a co-accused meant evidence which supported the prosecution case in a material respect or which undermined the defence of the co-accused,

- that, where it was established that a person jointly charged had given evidence against a co-accused, that co-accused had the right to cross-examine the other as to previous convictions, and the trial judge had no discretion to refuse an application to do so,

- that evidence against a co-accused might be given either in chief or during cross-cxamination,
- that it was to be objectively decided whether the evidence supported the prosecution case in a material respect or undermined the defence of the co-accused, hostile intent being irrelevant,
- that, where consideration had to be given to the question of whether the co-accused's defence was undermined, care had be taken to see that the evidence was clearly to that effect; inconvenience to, or inconsistency with, the co-accused's defence was not of itself sufficient,
- that a mere denial of participation in a joint venture was not of itself enough to rank as evidence against a co-accused. The denial had to lead to the conclusion that if the witness did not participate, then it must have been the other accused who did, and
- that, where one accused asserted a view of the joint venture which was directly contradicted by the other, that contradiction might be evidence against the co-accused.

The Court of Appeal found that on the facts before it, Varley's evidence was "evidence against" his co-accused, Dibble, because it not only contradicted the evidence of Dibble and amounted to an assertion that Dibble was lying, but also led to the conclusion that Dibble had participated in the crime on his own and had not acted under duress. It followed that the judge had been right to rule that cross-examination about Varley's previous convictions was permissible. The appeal was dismissed and Varley's conviction and sentence of 12 years' imprisonment confirmed. *R. v Joseph John Varley* (1982) 75 Cr. App. R. 242.

Commentary
These guidelines are consistent with the reasoned approach of Hederman J. in *McGrail*. Although that decision was concerned with the challenge to the character of prosecution witnesses opening the door to allowing cross-examination of the accused on previous convictions, whereas *Varley* was concerned with evidence given against a co-accused, the principle that emerges from both decisions is that not every assertion regarding character made by an accused automatically opens the door, but rather it is the impact of that assertion

which must justify allowing cross-examination.

Where imputations against the character of prosecution witnesses are "reasonably necessary" to establish a defence, they will not cause the door to be opened. On the other hand, where an imputation of bad character is unconnected with the proofs or the central issues of the case under consideration, the door is opened to allow cross-examination of the accused as to his or her character.

To adopt any other approach would prevent the accused from exercising his or her right to carry out a proper defence.

8. Hearsay Evidence

INTRODUCTION

A rule of evidence that often presents difficulties is the rule against hearsay. The principle of hearsay, and the rule against hearsay, is relatively straightforward. Problems arise with the exceptions to the rule and the application of the rule in certain situations.

Key Principle: If a witness testified as to what somebody told him outside court, that testimony is inadmissible if it seeks to prove the truth of what the witness was told, but it is admissible to prove that the witness had been told such a thing.

Subramaniam v Public Prosecutor [1956]

Subramaniam was found in a wounded state by members of the Malayan security forces operating against anti-government guerrillas. He was convicted of being in unlawful possession of ammunition (twenty .303 rounds) and sentenced to death. His appeal was turned down and he appealed to the Privy Council.

Subramaniam claimed that he had been captured by the guerrillas and was forced by them to carry ammunition, under duress and in fear of his life. He wanted to describe the words used by the guerrillas when they threatened his life, but the trial court disallowed such evidence, as the guerrillas were not in court to testify.

Held: The Privy Council held that the evidence of what the guerrillas had told Subramaniam was not hearsay as it was not offered in order to prove that what the guerrillas had said was true, but rather to prove that they had said something to him with the result that he acted under duress. The appeal was allowed and the decision of the Court of Appeal was reversed. *Subramaniam v Public Prosecutor on Appeal from the Supreme Court of the Federation of Malaya* [1956] 1 W.L.R. 965.

Key Principle: The primary reason for the rule is that evidence should be available for testing in the court. If a witness were allowed to repeat what another person said, it would be impossible to test that evidence unless the person who actually said those things was available for cross-examination. If the person who is supposed to have said such things is not in court, one of the most important methods of testing the truth and reliability of testimony is not available.

Re (In the matter of) Haughey [1971]

Pádraic Haughey was summoned by a committee of the Dáil to answer questions about alleged "gun-running" operations to Northern Ireland and the use of public funds to secure those arms. Hearsay evidence, containing serious accusations against Haughey, was received by the Committee.

Haughey attended as a witness but, having made a statement, he refused to answer any questions. As a result of this refusal, he was charged under the enabling Act and sentenced to six months' imprisonment. He appealed this conviction, which finally reached the Supreme Court.

Held: The Supreme Court held that the role of Haughey before the Committee was not that of a witness. He was accused of serious offences, and his conduct had become the subject matter of the Committee's enquiry and, accordingly, in those circumstances the enforcement of any rule of procedure which would deprive Haughey of his right to cross-examine, by counsel, his accusers, and to address, by counsel, the Committee in his defence, would violate the rights guaranteed by Article 40.3 of the Constitution. *In the matter of the Committee of Public Accounts of Dáil Éireann (Privilege and Procedure) Act of 1970, and in the matter of the Courts (Supplemental Provisions) Act of 1961, and in the matter of Pádraic (otherwise Páraic) Haughey* [1971] I.R. 217.

Key Principle: The exclusion of hearsay evidence and the emphasis on the process of cross-examination not only allows the court to hear the witness respond to searching questions, but it also allows the court to observe the behaviour of the witness (his demeanour), it ensures that the person who said the things is examined (best evidence), it prevents the introduction of previous consistent statements, and it prevents repetition of evidence and, therefore, keeps the trial as short as possible.

Teper v R. [1952]

Lejzor Teper was convicted of insurance fraud for deliberately setting fire to his shop. The Supreme Court of British Guiana turned down his appeal, and he appealed to the Privy Council.

At the trial, the evidence of a police constable was admitted for the purpose of identification. He testified: "I heard a woman's voice shouting 'Your place burning and you going away from the fire', immediately then a black car came from the direction of the fire, and in the car was a fair man resembling the accused. I did not observe the number of the car. I could not see the fire from where I was standing."

Under cross-examination, the constable admitted that he did not know who the woman was or where she was now.

Held: The Privy Council found that the evidence of what the woman said was hearsay and was so prejudicial to the accused that it deprived him of the substance of a fair trial. There was no other identification evidence of any value. The conviction was set aside. *Lejzor Teper v The Queen* [1952] A.C. 480.

Key Principle: The rule has often been criticised for being overly technical and not allowing evidence which is clearly relevant and has a high probative value.

R. v Gray [1841]

A dying person declared that he, and not the accused, had committed the murder. This deathbed confession was held to be hearsay evidence and inadmissible. *R. v Gray* (1841) 2 Cr. & Dix. 129.

Myers v DPP [1965]

Jimmy Myers was charged for stealing motorcars and reselling them with the logbooks of older cars. His alleged *modus operandi* was to steal cars and purchase identical wrecked cars. The stolen cars were thereafter sold after each one had been given the registration number of the wrecked car.

Myers admitted purchasing 12 wrecked cars and selling 12 cars bearing the same registration numbers as the wrecked cars, but he contended that the 12 wrecked cars had been repaired and rebuilt, and were not the stolen cars. He further claimed that in rebuilding the wrecked cars he had innocently removed the identification marks and plates and had replaced them on the rebuilt cars, so that the numbers registered in respect of those cars corresponded.

This meant that the prosecution had to prove that the cars and the logbooks did not belong together, and the only way they could do so was by showing that the number stamped on the cylinder block (which was hidden and had not been removed) did not match the logbook. These numbers had been stamped on the cylinder blocks by unidentified assembly line workers and recorded as such in the car manufacturer's records.

Held: The House of Lords disallowed the evidence of the cylinder block numbers because they were out of court assertions by unidentifiable workers. Myers' conviction was reversed. *James William Myers v Director of Public Prosecutions* [1965] A.C. 1001.

Commentary
It might be possible to justify the decision in *Gray*, as one could argue that if a person knew they were dying they might have motive to enable somebody to escape punishment for a crime. There are also instances of people confessing to crimes that they could never have committed, usually as a result of some psychological imbalance caused by a mental illness or by the process of dying.

The decision in *Myers,* however, is impossible to defend. It might be argued that the court needed to see and hear the automobile worker give evidence, just in case there was a mistake between the stamped number and the recorded number. However, given that Myers was charged with stealing 12 cars, it would have been highly improbable that all the block numbers were incorrect.

The House of Lords recognised the absurdity of the rule in this situation, but held that it was not their function to provide for exceptions and, therefore, legislative changes were needed. These changes were introduced almost immediately thereafter by the legislature in England in 1965 with the Criminal Evidence Act of 1965, replaced by the Criminal Justice Act of 1988 and amended by s.13 of the Civil Evidence Act of 1995.

In Ireland, a similar legislative enactment took the form of the Criminal Evidence Act of 1992. The Act contains an extended definition of "document", where a document would include (but not be limited to) items such as maps, plans, graphs, drawings, photographs and "any information in non-legible form reproduced in permanent legible form" (s.2) and Part II of the Act allows as evidence information in documentary form either compiled, or supplied, in the "ordinary course of business".

Key Principle: The exclusionary rule applies to both oral and written statements.

Cullen v Clarke [1963]

Peter Cullen, while employed as a builders' labourer, sustained injuries which left him with two flat feet and minor disabilities in his left foot, which made it necessary for him to walk with a stick. Although he was able to do some light work, he could no longer work as a builders' labourer, or take on any heavy work. He accordingly applied to have his partial disability treated as total incapacity.

At the Circuit Court hearing, Cullen gave evidence that he had applied for a number of jobs but had been refused work. He sought to give evidence of what was said to him by those to whom he applied, but this evidence was excluded as hearsay. Cullen's application for workmen's compensation was dismissed. He appealed to the Supreme Court.

Held: The Supreme Court held that Cullen was entitled to give evidence that when he had asked for work, the employers had said "no", but he was not allowed to give evidence of the reasons that they gave for their refusal. In giving evidence of their reasons, he was relying on the truth of such statements and, as such, the evidence was hearsay and the applicant would need the employers themselves to testify as to why they had not offered him work. The Supreme Court did, however, send the case back to the Circuit Court with the recommendation that where the workman's work record is good and there was no slump in the labour market, a judge was entitled to find that a workman's partial incapacity should be treated as total in the appropriate circumstances. *In the matter of the Workmen's Compensation Acts, 1934–1955, Peter Cullen v William Clarke* [1963] I.R. 368.

Commentary

When the evidence is tendered to show that words were spoken, that is direct evidence and is admissible. Accordingly, the evidence that the employers had said "no" was direct evidence.

However, when Cullen sought to go further by leading evidence to show that the employers had said "no" because of his injuries, this was hearsay as it supplied the reason for their refusal, and only the employers themselves could testify as to their reasons for saying "no" to Cullen.

Key Principle: There is uncertainty regarding the hearsay status of so-called "implied assertions"—in other words, where the words are not tendered as evidence of what they assert, but rather what they imply. It would seem that the majority opinion is that implied assertions must be treated on the same basis as express assertions— if they imply the truth of the contents of an out-of-court statement, they are hearsay.

Ratten v R. [1972]

Leith Ratten was convicted of the murder of his wife by shooting her with a shotgun. His defence was that the gun had discharged accidentally whilst he was cleaning it.

To rebut that defence the prosecution called evidence from a telephone operator, Miss Flowers, who stated that shortly before the time of the shooting, she had received a call from the address where the deceased woman lived with her husband, Ratten. The voice was a female one, clearly hysterical and punctuated by heavy sobbing, who said: "Get me the police, please!" and thereafter supplied her address. The operator testified that before she could connect the call to the police station, the woman hung up.

Ratten objected to that evidence as being hearsay, in that it was being led to show that something was happening in the house, namely that the deceased was being attacked or was under threat by him. The prosecution argued that it was being led to show that the words were said and was, therefore, direct evidence. Ratten was convicted.

Ratten applied to the Supreme Court of Victoria (Australia) for leave to appeal against conviction but his application was dismissed. He further appealed to the Privy Council.

Held: The Privy Council held that words spoken are facts just as much as any other action by a human being. If the speaking of words is a relevant fact, a witness may give evidence that they were spoken. A question of hearsay only arises when the words spoken are relied on to establish some fact as narrated by the words. If, however, the words are being tendered as evidence of an assertion (in this case an assertion by the deceased that she was being attacked by Ratten), then it was being put forward as evidence of the truth of the facts being asserted by the statement, and accordingly was hearsay. *Leith McDonald Ratten v R.* [1972] A.C. 378.

However, the Privy Council held that the evidence of the receptionist could be admitted as original evidence as it rebutted Ratten's assertion that no telephone call was made from his house at the time of the shot and it also rebutted his claim that the shotgun had fired accidentally, as the deceased had clearly been in a distressed state prior to her death. Therefore, the utterance of the words was the evidence, rather than their content or implication.

R. v Kearley [1992]

Alan Kearley was charged with possessing illegal drugs for the purposes of supply. At the trial, the prosecution was allowed to lead evidence that, following Kearley's arrest, and not in his presence or hearing, a number of telephone calls had been made to his house in which the callers requested to speak to him and asked for drugs. Evidence was also led that a number of people had physically visited Kearley's house and asked for drugs. None of these persons were called to give evidence. Kearley objected that this evidence was hearsay.

Held: (by a majority of three against two) by the House of Lords, that so far as the callers' requests could be treated as having impliedly asserted that Kearley was a supplier of drugs, evidence of the requests was excluded by the rule against hearsay, since that rule applied equally to implied as to express assertions, and the fact that a multiplicity of requests for drugs might have greater probative force than a single request was not a ground for disregarding the rule (as was argued by the judges in the minority). *R. v Alan Robert Michael Kearley* [1992] 2 W.L.R. 656).

Commentary

In both cases, the prosecution sought to draw inferences from out-of-court statements, and those inferences were, accordingly, deemed hearsay evidence. This issue was clear enough in *Ratten,* where the evidence was admitted as original evidence to rebut a defence, rather than as hearsay evidence to prove the truth of a statement.

However, in *Kearley,* the fact that a number of people believed that they could get drugs from him was held to be irrelevant to the issues before the court. Of course, it could be argued that the fact that a lot of people called and all believed that Kearley would supply them with drugs raised the probative value of the evidence, but the majority argued that the principle could not change just because the evidence was about the state of mind of a lot of people rather than the state of mind of just one person—what was being excluded was the state-of-mind evidence, and the number of times it occurred did not change the nature of the evidence.

Whilst this decision is correct in principle, it seems to contradict another principle that evidence should be admitted where its probative value outweighs its prejudicial effect. In other words, following *Ratten*, could it not be argued that the number of telephone calls and visits by people asking for drugs was direct evidence of the accused's guilt as it established that there were a lot of people expecting to buy drugs from the accused?

The *res gestae*

Key Principle: Where a statement is so intertwined with an act under consideration that it can be said to be part of the act, evidence of that statement may be admissible despite it being an out-of-court statement, particularly if it is only possible to make sense of the act in conjunction with the statement. This statement is known as the *res gestae*.

R. v Bedingfield [1879]

Henry Bedingfield's girlfriend would not succumb to his amorous advances, and he wished to end the relationship. Evidence was led that he had threatened to cut her throat. She was scared and asked a policeman to keep an eye on her house.

The policeman testified that on the morning in question, Bedingfield and his girlfriend were together in her house for some time. He had heard the voice of a man raised in anger. Bedingfield had left to buy alcohol and thereafter returned to the house. A short time later, the woman came out of the house with her throat cut. She said something to her two assistants and pointed back towards the house, before falling down dead.

Bedingfield's defence was that the deceased woman had first cut his throat and then her own.

Held: The Crown Court held that the statement made by the deceased was hearsay and could not be tendered in evidence. It was not part of the *res gestae* "for it was not part of anything done, or something said while something was being done, but something said after something was done". Despite this, the medical evidence was conclusive that she had not committed suicide, and Bedingfield was found guilty and hanged. *R. v Henry Bedingfield* (1879) 14 Cox C.C. 341.

Commentary
The difficulty with the concept of *res gestae* is determining when the transaction or the act under consideration starts and ends, and whether the statement forms part of that transaction or action.

It can be stated as a principle of law that the doctrine of *res gestae*, as an exception to the hearsay rule, encompasses four similar but distinct situations:

1. Spontaneous statements made by a participant in an act;
2. Spontaneous statements which accompany and explain an act;
3. Spontaneous statements which explain the state of mind of the person making the statement at the relevant time;
4. Spontaneous statements which describe the physical sensations felt by the maker of the statement at the relevant time.

The similarity of the situations is evident. The statement must be contemporaneous with the relevant act under consideration, the maker of the statement cannot, or is not called to, give evidence, and the content of the statements is led as proof of the truth of their contents, as opposed to merely proving that statements were made.

Key Principle: The element of contemporaneousness which was so important in early cases like Bedingfield, has been relaxed somewhat in later cases, on the supposition that what is said "in the heat of the moment" is likely to be true, even though it is not strictly part of the action or transaction under consideration.

R. v Andrews [1987]

Alexander Morrow was attacked, stabbed and robbed by two men in his flat. Within minutes of the attack, and bleeding profusely from a deep stomach wound, he raised the alarm, and the police soon arrived. Morrow stated that he had been attacked by two men, one called Peter O'Neill and the other he knew as Donald. The policeman wrote this in his diary, recording the name as "Donovan" rather than "Donald". Morrow died two months later.

Peter O'Neill and Donald Andrews were both charged with the murder. At the trial the judge allowed the prosecution to lead the evidence of what Morrow had told the policeman under the *res gestae* exception, despite the defence objecting that it was hearsay. Andrews was convicted. The Court of Appeal confirmed the finding and the matter was appealed to the House of Lords.

Held: The House of Lords held that the evidence of the conversation could be admitted under the *res gestae* doctrine where the possibility of concoction or distortion can be disregarded. The trial judge must consider whether the circumstances in which the statement was made were so unusual, startling or dramatic as to dominate the thoughts of the declarant so that his utterance was an instinctive reaction to the event rather than reasoned reflection. The statement can be admitted even where it is made in conditions of approximate, but not exact, contemporaneousness where the declarant's mind is still dominated by the event. The statement must be closely associated with the event. If there were a possibility of error, this would go to the weight of the evidence, which was a matter to be considered by the jury once the judge had declared the evidence admissible. The appeal was dismissed. *The Queen v Donald Joseph Andrews* [1987] WL 492116.

Commentary
This judgment stripped away a lot of the artificiality associated with the hearsay rule. The House of Lords even went so far as to say that they thought *Bedingfield* was wrongly decided.

DECLARATIONS MADE BY PEOPLE SINCE DECEASED

Statements made by people since deceased are admissible under certain circumstances, and provided that the evidence would be admissible if the person was alive to testify in the usual fashion.

Dying declarations

A dying declaration is made by a person who thinks that they are about to die ("a settled and hopeless expectation of death"). It is not necessary for the declarant to die immediately after making the statement, only that they think they are about to die when they make the statement.

These statements are only admissible in murder and manslaughter cases and must be led in an attempt to establish the cause of death and the identity of the killer.

Key Principle: The declarant must have a settled and hopeless expectation of death.

R. v Jenkins (1869)

Henry Jenkins was convicted of the murder of Fanny Reeves, who had named him as her murderer in a statement made under oath to a magistrate's clerk.

The clerk asked Fanny if she felt she was likely to die? She replied, "I think so". He asked her why she thought she was about to die? She replied, "From the shortness of my breath". He asked her, "Is it with the fear of death before you that you make these statements?" He went on, "Have you any present hope of recovery?" to which she replied "None".

In her statement Fanny described how she had asked Jenkins for money, as he was the father of her first child. He did not have the money, and an argument ensued. Jenkins had walked over to the river bank and had told her to come and look at a rat climbing up the bank. She had peered over the bank, but could not see any rat. Jenkins had shouted, "Take that, you bugger" and had shoved her in the back so that she fell into the River Avon. She had managed to keep herself above water by holding onto the bank and had screamed until she was rescued by a policeman. She lost consciousness and awoke in bed, and since then "felt great pain in my chest, bosom and back".

The clerk thereafter wrote out her statement, and asked her if it was correct. She asked him to insert the words, "No hope, at present, of my recovery", and he inserted those words.

Held: The declaration was inadmissible, as by inserting the words "at present" the deceased was qualifying her previous statement that she had no hope of recovery. She was "not in that hopeless state of impending death that was necessary to render her declaration admissible in evidence". As her statement was the only evidence against Jenkins, his conviction was overturned. *R. v Henry Jenkins* (1869) 11 Cox C.C. 250.

Commentary
The rationale for this exception is that a person would not want to die with a lie on his or her lips. In most religions, to die in such a manner would exclude the possibility of redemption and would therefore result in eternal damnation. Again, it is unclear whether this rationale can be justified in light of what we now know about the human psyche, and the fact that a lot of people no longer believe in a Divine Being. As a result, this exception has become a rather controversial one.

Another problematic aspect of this exception is the difficulty in showing that the declarant knew that he or she was about to die and had accepted that fact. In *Andrews*, where the declarant identified his killers to the police and died of his wounds thereafter, the statement was not allowed as a dying declaration, as it could not be shown that the declarant knew that he was about to die. (He, in fact, died two months later). However, the statement was allowed under the *res gestae* exception as there was little chance of "concoction and distortion".

In *Jenkins*, the exception would seem to be at its most artificial, with the decision resting essentially on semantics and the deceased's choice of words shortly before her death. Following *Andrews*, if the same facts came before a court today, it must be argued that such declarations should be admissible if the possibility of concoction and distortion can be safely disregarded.

DECLARATIONS AGAINST PROPRIETARY OR PECUNIARY INTEREST

If a person makes a statement against their interest, that statement can be admitted as evidence despite the maker not being able to testify to it.

Key Principle: A statement made by a person since deceased can be admitted as evidence where that statement is shown to be against the maker's proprietary or pecuniary interest.

Flood v Russell (1891)

In a dispute about the existence of a will, the wife of the testator stated that her husband had indeed made a will and had left her a life estate in certain property.

Held: As the deceased's wife, the declarant was entitled to more than just the life estate if his estate was declared intestate. Accordingly, her statement was against her proprietary and pecuniary interest, and was, therefore, admissible. *Flood v Russell* (1891) 29 L.R.Ir. 91.

Commentary
Here the rationale is logically defensible: the statement is more than likely to be true as there is no incentive to lie against yourself.

DECLARATIONS MADE IN THE COURSE OF DUTY

Key Principle: A declaration made by a person in the course of a duty owed to somebody else, can be admitted after the declarant's death.

Harris v Lambert HC [1932]

Lambert H.C. were the executors of a deceased estate, and resisted a claim by Harris for an amount of £21,506 4s. 3d., which Harris claimed was due to him under a family deed of settlement.

Lambert sought to prove that the deed of settlement did not transfer the money to Harris, that it was executed as a result of a mistake, and that it should be rectified. They sought to lead evidence of entries made in the diary of a Mr Giltrap, who had been their solicitor, but who had since died. The entries were a record of interviews with a Mr Mills, the English solicitor for Harris, in regard to the proposed settlement.

Harris objected to the evidence being admitted, arguing that Giltrap had made the entries solely for the purpose of drawing his costs, and not in pursuance of a duty to his client. Lambert argued that it was part of the duty of the solicitor to keep a record of what transpired at interviews on his client's behalf. He had to advise his client as to the nature of the interviews, and to refresh his memory as to what occurred at those interviews, and, accordingly, the entries were admissible.

Held: The notes were admissible in evidence as they were made for the primary purpose of having a record of what happened at the interviews and in regard to the negotiations, which extended over a considerable period, and were necessary to allow the solicitor to properly carry out his duties to his client, namely deciding whether to approve (or not) the family settlement. *Harris and others v Lambert and another* [1932] I.R. 504.

Commentary
The rationale for this exception is perhaps dubious: the assumption is that a person would not lie where the information is made or recorded for the purposes of work.

DECLARATIONS MADE BY A TESTATOR

Key Principle: Declarations made by a testator since deceased which explain the contents of his will are admissible only if they are necessary to explain the contents of his will.

Goods of Ball (1890)

The testator wrote on the first page of a copy of his will that he had substituted the copy for the original.

Held: This statement was admitted to prove the contents of the will. *Goods of Ball* (1890) 25 L.R. Ir. 556.

Commentary
Clearly where the will is straightforward, the comments of the testator are irrelevant and, therefore, inadmissible.

DECLARATIONS OF PEDIGREE

Key Principle: Declarations made by a deceased person relating to a matter of pedigree (for example the date of birth or death of somebody, a date of marriage, or whether a birth was intramarital or extramarital) are sometimes admissible. The person making the declaration has to be a blood relative, or the spouse of a blood relative, of the person who was the subject of the declaration. The declaration has to be made before the dispute concerning the issue of pedigree arose.

Re Holmes (In the matter of): Beamish v Smeltzer [1934]

During an inquiry to establish the next-of-kin of the late George W. Holmes, the decision of the case rested ultimately on "the affidavit of Mrs Hannah Switzer, an old lady of about ninety years of age, and the evidence both written and oral of Matthew Deeves, who is 83 years of age", neither being members of the family of the deceased. The objection was taken that, as it was a declaration of pedigree, the evidence could only be given by a member of the deceased's family.

Held: The testimony contained in Mrs Switzer's affidavit was entirely within her own knowledge, and was not hearsay. The testimony of Mr Deeves consisted partly of his own knowledge and partly of declarations of deceased members of the family made to him, and was accordingly admissible. *In the matter of the Estate of George W. Holmes, deceased: Caroline Beamish v John Smeltzer* [1934] I.R. 693.

Commentary

Curiously, there was no need to prove that the declarant had personal knowledge of the issue. The rationale for this exception is that family members would speak the truth amongst themselves regarding issues of pedigree as there was nothing to be gained by lying.

The principle established in *Re Holmes*, that the declarant must be a blood relation of the deceased whereas the witness testifying about the declaration need not be, seems to contradict the original (and already dubious) rationale that family members would speak the truth amongst themselves regarding issues of pedigree as there was nothing to be gained by lying. Even if this shaky logic was true, why would the declarant not lie to a potential witness who was not a member of the family?

STATEMENTS IN PUBLIC DOCUMENTS

Under certain conditions, statements in public documents are admissible to prove the facts that they contain. The document must be made by a public officer (a civil servant) for the public, with the intention that the public can, and will, use the document.

Key Principle: The statement in a public document constitutes prima facie proof only. Accordingly, it creates a rebuttable presumption that the facts contained in the document are true.

Kiely v Minister for Social Welfare [1977]

Section 16 of the Welfare (Occupational Injuries) Act of 1966 states that a death benefit shall be payable where an insured person suffers from injuries "caused ... by accident" arising out of, and in the course of, his insurable employment.

Louisa Kiely's husband was severely burnt at work. He died two years later from a coronary thrombosis. Mrs Kiely made a claim for death benefit on the basis that the stress and anxiety experienced by her husband due to his injuries had induced the fatal thrombosis. The claim was rejected by a deciding officer and, on appeal, by an appeals officer.

At the hearing before the appeals officer, two doctors gave oral evidence on behalf of Mrs Kiely to the effect that the deceased's injuries had been a cause of his death. Their evidence was contradicted by a letter from another doctor who had been briefed by an official of the Department of Social Welfare.

Mrs Kiely disputed the introduction of the letter as it was hearsay. The Minister for Social Welfare argued that it was admissible under the exception that the letter had been prepared for public scrutiny. The High Court allowed the evidence and dismissed the appeal. Mrs Kiely appealed to the Supreme Court.

Held: The Supreme Court held that the appeals officer had acted without jurisdiction in allowing the proof of Mrs Kiely's claim furnished by the oral evidence of her witnesses to be rebutted by the written statement of the absent witness. It is an infringement of the requirements of natural justice to require one party to a dispute to attend the hearing of proceedings for the purposes of leading oral evidence in support of her claim and, at the same time, to allow the opposing party to controvert that oral evidence by furnishing a written statement made by a witness who does not attend the hearing. The appeal was upheld. *In the matter of the Social Welfare Act, 1952: Louisa Kiely v the Minister for Social Welfare* [1977] I.R. 267.

Commentary

The rationale for this exception is that a public officer will always carry out his or her duties diligently if they expect their work to be subject to public scrutiny—hence, the requirement that the document must have been prepared for public scrutiny.

This common-law exception has been largely replaced by similar statutory exceptions which declare that the contents of certain public documents are to be regarded as prima facie proof of their contents. The courts can always overrule these statutory exceptions if they are used to subvert the principles of natural justice.

Examples would be the Registration of Births and Deaths (Ireland) Act of 1883, the Marriages (Ireland) Act of 1844, the Bankers Books Evidence Act of 1879 and 1959 (which all exempt certain certificates produced in court as evidence), the Criminal Evidence Act of 1992 (which allows the contents of a document made in the ordinary course of business to be admitted as evidence in criminal proceedings—largely as a result of the *Myers v DPP* decision), and the Children Act of 1997 (admitting a prior statement made by a child where the court considers that the child is unable to give evidence by reason of age or where it would not be in the child's best interests to give *viva voce* evidence—largely as a result of the decision of in *Re M., S. and W.*).

THE WAY FORWARD FOR THE HEARSAY RULE

Key Principle: The rule against hearsay is a judge-made rule and, as such, can be changed or adapted by the courts where circumstances demand it.

Re M., S. and W. [1996]

The Eastern Health Board (EHB) instituted proceedings to make three children wards of court on the grounds that at least one of the children had been sexually abused by their father. The EHB did not call the child to give evidence but sought to lead evidence of what the child had said to a speech therapist and a social worker during interviews. The interview with the social worker was recorded on video. The video-recording of the interview was shown to the court with the consent of the parents, but the parents objected to the admission of the evidence of the social worker, on the basis that such evidence was hearsay evidence.

Held: The High Court allowed the evidence of the social worker about the interview, including his comments on the video. Costello J. found that the rule against the admission of hearsay evidence was a judge-made rule which has never been strictly applied in wardship proceedings. The court was acting as *parens* *patriae* (the guardian and protector of all children) when it exercised its jurisdiction in wardship proceedings. In exercising this jurisdiction, the courts have always acted in the best interests of the child. The non-applicability of the hearsay rule was justified by the nature of the jurisdiction exercised by the court. This was an investigative jurisdiction to ensure the best interests of the child, rather than a purely adversarial jurisdiction where the judge was no more than a referee. This judgment was upheld by the Supreme Court. *Re M., S. and W., infants* [1996] 1 I.L.R.M. 370.

Commentary
In the usual course of events, for example, if the question of the social worker giving evidence about what the child told him arose during the criminal trial of the father, it is doubtful whether the court would have allowed that evidence, and the prosecution would have been forced to lead the child in evidence. For that reason, if there was no other evidence available, the DPP might well have declined to prosecute. However, this was not a criminal trial, but a wardship hearing. The court adapted the rules of evidence to fulfil its specific function, namely, to protect the child, rather than establish the guilt or innocence of the alleged offender.

9. Confessions

INTRODUCTION

One of the most controversial exceptions to the rule against hearsay is the confession. Confessions are regarded as an exception to the hearsay rule because they are statements made against self-interest, the rationale being that nobody will fabricate testimony that is damaging to them.

However, there is a contradiction in the rationale. Why would a person accused of a crime make a statement against his interests? The answer would often seem to be that the confessor did not make the statement voluntarily and, therefore, it is the question of voluntariness that the court will initially scrutinise.

Ideally, confessions should be in the form of a written statement, perhaps supported by a video-tape of the interview. However, there is no absolute prohibition on oral confessions, and the form of the confession will determine its weight, as opposed to its admissibility.

Key Principle: If a confession was not given voluntarily, it is inadmissible. The trial judge has no discretion to allow it. Where challenged, the burden is on the prosecution to establish beyond reasonable doubt that a confession is voluntary.

R. v Thompson [1893]

Marcellus Thompson was charged with embezzling the money of a company. Evidence was led that when challenged by the chairman of the company, he said, "Yes, I took the money," and made out a list of the embezzled sums and, with the assistance of his brother, repaid a portion of the stolen moneys to the company. In his evidence, the chairman testified that no threat was used and no promise made as regards Thompson's prosecution. He did admit that he had said to Thompson's brother, "It will be the right thing for your brother to make a statement." The Court drew the inference that Thompson knew that the chairman had said this to his brother when he confessed.

Held: The confession had not been proved to be free and voluntary and, therefore, evidence of the confession was inadmissible. *R. v Marcellus Thompson* [1893] 2 Q.B. 12.

Commentary
In addition to the confession, there was considerable evidence against Thompson, but his conviction was quashed.

Perhaps a clue to the court's benevolence was the fact that he showed remorse at the time, and had repaid a large portion of the stolen money at the time of the trial. However, it also underlines the importance placed on the voluntariness of the confession, to the extent that the involuntary confession tainted the remainder of the investigation and subsequent proceedings.

This conforms with the general principle of Irish law that the prosecution must provide independent proof of the accused's guilt.

Key Principle: Confessions obtained by inducements (threats or promises) made by persons in authority can be excluded.

Attorney-General v Cleary (1934)

Bridget Cleary was charged with infanticide following the murder of her newborn baby. She was a married woman with five children by her husband. The child in question resulted from an affair with her employer's son.

The evidence was that Cleary had unsuccessfully attempted to gain admission to the local infirmary. She spent the night at her employer's house and gave birth in an outlying barn. The medical evidence was that the child was born alive, but shortly thereafter was killed by being strangled with a piece of rope.

Cleary testified that she lost consciousness after the birth and, while denying that she had killed the child, she could give very little account of how the child had died. The child's body was discovered wrapped in a pillowcase and buried in her employer's garden.

The basis of the prosecution's case was a written statement made to a Garda Sergeant who supposedly cautioned Cleary at the time. As a result of her statement, the body of the dead infant was discovered. The written statement was the only evidence that connected Cleary to the baby's death.

Cleary denied that the Sergeant had cautioned her, and claimed to be unaware that she did not have to make a statement. In addition, the evidence indicated that the Sergeant had said to her that he would bring the doctor to her, and she had taken this to mean that the truth of any statement she made would be tested by a medical examination.

The trial judge decided that her fear was not sufficient to affect the truth of the statement, and it was admitted as evidence.

Cleary appealed her conviction.

Held: The question of whether the truth lies one way or another does not matter. Similarly, the nature of the inducement, whether fear or offer of reward or whatever it may have been, is not a matter which determines the admissibility of a statement. The sole question of admissibility is whether the confession was made voluntarily. As Cleary was clearly in a state of terror when she made the statement, it could not be said to be voluntary, and should not have been admitted.

As the prosecution had withheld certain other evidence against Cleary once her statement was admitted, the court quashed the conviction but ordered a retrial on a charge of manslaughter. *Attorney-General v Bridget K. Cleary* (1934) 1 Frewen 14.

Commentary
It is often difficult to separate the two enquiries, but the voluntariness of the confession must be established before the truth of the confession can be assessed. This makes sense when one realises that it is only once the evidence of the confession is before the court that the question becomes whether it is the truth or not—in other words, it is only then that the weight of the evidence is assessed.

The initial enquiry, before the weight of the confession is assessed, determines whether it should be allowed into the court at all in order to assess it.

Key Principle: The trial judge must decide whether the person making the inducements was a person in authority.

DPP v McCann [1998]

Francis McCann was convicted of murder for starting the fire that killed his wife and foster-daughter and was sentenced to life imprisonment.

The evidence against McCann was strong. The prosecution showed how he had concocted a number of threats, supposedly made against him as proprietor of a public house, "with arson as the prominent ingredient". By doing this he hoped to be able to blame another person for the fire.

The prosecution claimed that the motive for the murder was connected with difficulties McCann was facing regarding the adoption of his foster-daughter. The adoption agency had discovered that he had fathered a child with a young girl. The prosecution claimed that he had decided to kill his wife before this news got to her.

McCann was arrested but denied any involvement in the fire and refused to answer any questions put to him about the explosion. At about 3.34 p.m. he was visited by his solicitor, and thereafter refused to say anything on the advice of his solicitor.

The next day he was interviewed again, but remained silent. On the following day, however, he admitted to concocting and creating the threatening messages and calls. He was asked why he would not talk of the fire, and became very distressed. Bernard and Michael, his brothers, had met with him on the previous day, when he told them that he and his wife had discussed a suicide pact.

In the presence of Detective Sergeant Glennon, the brothers asked McCann to repeat what he had told them. This he did, in the presence of the investigating officer, his two brothers, and his solicitor. He admitted to starting the fire, and described exactly what he had done with the petrol and matches, and where he had started the fire.

At that stage, Sergeant Flynn entered the interview room and told McCann that he was released under the provisions of s.30 of the Offences Against the State Act 1939. His original detention had been extended from 24 hours to 48 hours, but the extended time expired at 1.22 p.m. Despite this, McCann returned a couple of minutes later and the interview continued at 1.29 p.m. with the same parties present. McCann continued to describe how he had started the fire, and thereafter signed the notes of this interview as did those others present. This statement was admitted as evidence at the trial.

At his appeal, McCann argued that this statement was inadmissible due to the oppressive circumstances of his detention and he further argued that the trial judge was wrong in finding that his brothers were not persons in authority when they induced him to speak.

Held: The Court of Criminal Appeal found that the admissions that were made happened during the extended time of McCann's detention. He had had the advice of two solicitors at different times throughout his detention. He was visited by two doctors, and he was allowed to take mild relaxants. He was given an opportunity to sleep and was provided with food and drink.

There was no evidence that his brothers had attempted to influence him in any way. The most that had happened was that Bernard had urged him to tell the truth and to protect the reputation of their family.

As to what constitutes an inducement, the test was:

- Were the words used by the person or persons in authority, objectively viewed, capable of amounting to a threat or promise?
- Did the accused subjectively understand them as such?
- Was his confession in fact the result of the threat or promise?

Regarding the question of whether the brothers could be said to be "persons in authority", the court found that this has always been held to mean someone engaged in the arrest, detention, examination or prosecution of the accused, or someone acting on behalf of the prosecution. This did not properly describe the role of his brothers. In the circumstances, the confession was admissible. The appeal was refused. *The People (at the suit of the Director of Public Prosecutions) v Francis McCann* [1998] 4 I.R. 397.

Key Principle: The use of oppression or oppressive questioning can cause a confession to be deemed involuntary.

DPP v Lynch [1982]

Christopher Lynch, who was a gunner in the army, had been asked to paint and decorate the interior of a house. With this in mind, Lynch entered the house at 12.00 noon on Sunday. Upon entering the house, he discovered the dead body of a woman, Vera Cooney, who had lived in the top flat of the house. A knife was embedded in her chest and a scarf was tightly bound around her neck. Lynch called the Gardaí, and at 4.00 p.m. he went to the station to make a statement. He completed the statement at 7.45 p.m. on that Sunday.

In the statement Lynch described how he had found the deceased and stated that he had been in the house on the previous day, the Saturday. Lynch remained in the station for the remainder of that Sunday night and he was questioned almost continually from 1.30 a.m. until 8.30 a.m. on Monday. At 10.00 a.m. he was brought to another Garda station where he was interrogated until 2.00 p.m., when he confessed to the murder. Having slept for a few hours, he was awakened at 6.00 p.m. and completed a written statement confessing that he had killed the woman at some time before 2.30 p.m. on Saturday.

Near the beginning of this last two-hour period, Lynch's wife, with her baby, arrived at the station. She demanded to see her husband, but was refused. Lynch remained in one room with Garda Kenny and Garda Murphy while his wife, without his knowledge, was kept in another room in the same building.

The confession was the sole basis of the case for the prosecution.

During the trial, it emerged that the woman had been seen alive some considerable time after Lynch said he had killed her. In addition, Lynch said he had strangled her with a piece of wire, whereas she had been strangled with a scarf. The trial judge found that the confession had not been procured through fear or promise and was, therefore, admissible. The jury returned a verdict of guilty.

Lynch appealed directly to the Supreme Court against his conviction.

Held: The Supreme Court held that although the trial judge had found Lynch's admission of guilt to be voluntary, he should have excluded the confession in the exercise of his general discretion since the circumstances of its procurement had been oppressive. The fact that Lynch was subjected to sustained questioning for almost 22 hours, was prevented from communicating with his family or friends, and was not permitted to rest or sleep until he confessed all amounted to such circumstances of harassment and oppression as to make it unjust and unfair to admit in evidence anything he said. As there was no other evidence against Lynch apart from these statements, his conviction was quashed. *The People (at the suit of the Director of Public Prosecutions) v Christopher Anthony Lynch* [1982] I.R. 64.

DPP v Shaw [1982]

John Shaw and Geoffrey Evans were arrested by the Gardaí on a Sunday, without a warrant, for being in possession of a stolen motor car. The men were suspected of being responsible for the disappearance of two young women: Elizabeth, who had disappeared in Wicklow a month earlier, and Mary, who had disappeared in Mayo four days earlier.

The Gardaí were anxious for the safety of the two women and, with this in mind, wished to keep the men in custody for as long as possible. Accordingly, although there was a sitting of the District Court on Monday morning, Shaw was not brought before the court at this first opportunity. The questioning of both men continued on Monday until Evans confessed on Monday evening and, in so doing, incriminated Shaw in the murder of Elizabeth. On Tuesday morning, Shaw signed a written statement in which he admitted to killing Mary. That afternoon, Shaw was driven to the place where he said he had killed Mary and burnt or hidden her clothes.

On Wednesday, Shaw was brought before Wicklow District Court and charged with the murder, rape and false imprisonment of Mary. He was convicted of these offences after a trial in the Central Criminal Court. His statement was admitted as evidence as the trial judge was satisfied that because of the reasonable and genuine concern of the Gardaí for the safety of the two missing girls, the continued detention of the accused did not amount to a conscious and deliberate violation of the accused's constitutional rights and, even if it did, there were extraordinary excusatory circumstances within the meaning of the exception laid down in *O'Brien*'s case.

Shaw appealed his conviction. The Court of Criminal Appeal agreed with the finding and reasoning of the trial judge, and turned down the appeal. However, the Court of Criminal Appeal recognised that the case involved a point of law of exceptional public importance and referred the matter to the Supreme Court.

Held: The Supreme Court held that despite being initially arrested for the possession of a stolen motor car, the detention of Shaw became lawful when he was informed of the true reason for his detention. In the special circumstances, his continued detention was justified and lawful, as the Gardaí had endeavoured to protect the more important of two conflicting constitutional rights, the right to life versus the right to liberty and were, accordingly, justified in their actions. Finally, as the statements of the two men were made voluntarily, they were properly admitted by the trial judge. The Supreme Court confirmed the conviction. *The People (at the suit of the Director of Public Prosecutions) v John Shaw* [1982] I.R. 1.

Key Principle: It is not only threats or promises that can render a confession involuntary. The conditions under which questioning occurs must also be considered.

DPP v McNally & Breathnach (1981)

Brian McNally and Osgur Breathnach were convicted by the Special Criminal Court of carrying out the Sallins train robbery. The only evidence against them was confessions they had made whilst in custody. Breathnach made his confession after being in custody for approximately 40 hours. During that time, he was interrogated extensively, allowed very little sleep and was denied access to his solicitor. When awakened from a brief rest, he was further interrogated in the passageway of the Bridewell Garda Station in Dublin. He finally made a confession at 4.00 a.m.

Held: The Court of Criminal Appeal held that these circumstances were oppressive and the confession inadmissible, as this treatment had sapped his will and made his confession involuntary. *The People (at the suit of the Director of Public Prosecutions) v Brian McNally & Osgur Breathnach* (1981) 2 Frewen 43.

Key Principle: When deciding on the voluntariness, or otherwise, of a confession, the inquiry is what effect the inducement or threat had upon the person to whom it was put, and not what was intended or hoped for by the person in authority.

DPP v Hoey [1987]

Anthony Hoey's house was raided by the Gardaí, who found a revolver, a pistol and ammunition, together with balaclavas and gloves. Hoey was in the house when the Gardaí arrived at the front door but he ran out the back door and remained "on the run" for over three months until he turned himself in at Bridewell Garda Station, Dublin, accompanied by his solicitor. He was detained in terms of s.30 of the Offences Against the State Act 1939.

Hoey was interviewed by members of the Gardaí for three hours and was thereafter given a break and the offer of a meal, which he declined. He spoke on the telephone to his solicitor for about five minutes at 9.30 p.m., and again at 9.30 a.m. after having a sleep. Between 10.30 p.m. and 11.00 p.m. on that first day, Hoey made a statement in the presence of Detective Inspector Anders and Detective Garda Fitzpatrick in which he accepted responsibility for the guns and ammunition found at 78 Rossmore Avenue, Ballyfermot. This statement was the only evidence connecting Hoey with the discovered firearms and ammunition.

Hoey was convicted for being in illegal possession of arms and ammunition and appealed to the Criminal Appeal Court.

The main basis of Hoey's appeal was that his confession was inadmissible, as he had confessed after the investigating officer had said to him:

"Will I have to get some member to go up to your family and find out from them if anybody at 78 Rossmore Avenue is going to take responsibility for the property in the house?"

The Court of Criminal Appeal found that the statement was voluntary in the sense that it was not extracted from him by any improper inducement containing threat or promise of temporal disadvantage or advantage and in the sense that it was an act of his free will, such as to be his own voluntary statement. The application for leave to appeal was refused but the matter was forwarded to the Supreme Court as involving points of law of exceptional public importance.

Held: The Supreme Court allowed the appeal and set aside the conviction. The court found that the prosecution had not proved the statement to have been free and voluntary. Hoey had been unwilling to make any statement until the question was put to him about his family, and it was clear beyond all reasonable doubt that the effect of the question was to cause him to make the confession. In the circumstances of the case, that amounted to an improper inducement.

The onus was on the prosecution to prove that the statement was voluntary, the test being whether or not the question was calculated to induce the confessor to admit the offence because of fear of prejudice or hope of advantage. The test was an objective one and it was irrelevant to consider the intention or motive of the person who posed the question. *The People (at the suit of the Director of Public Prosecutions) v Anthony Hoey* [1987] I.R. 637.

Key Principle: There must be a causal link between the threat, inducement or oppression and the confession made.

DPP v Ward [2002]

Paul Ward was believed by the Gardaí to be the mastermind behind the murder of the journalist Veronica Guerin. He was charged and convicted of her murder before the Special Criminal Court and received a sentence of life imprisonment.

The evidence was that during five sessions of interrogation totalling fourteen and a half hours, Ward remained silent. On the evening of the second day of his detention, Ward was visited by his partner, Vanessa Meehan. She had been arrested by the Gardaí and it was they who brought her to visit him, without any request from Ward. That visit lasted for one hour and Ward was then further interrogated at 10.35 p.m., at which point he admitted to planning the killing and disposing of the murder weapons thereafter.

On appeal, Ward argued that the visit by Vanessa Meehan and a subsequent visit by his 74-year-old mother, which were arranged by the Gardaí without his knowledge, constituted unfair oppression which amounted to a conscious and deliberate violation of his right to fair procedures.

Held: The Court of Criminal Appeal found that the admissions made by Ward (if such admissions were made, as there was evidence to suggest that the confession had not occurred but had been entirely fabricated) were induced by grievous psychological pressure which affected the free will of Ward to such an extent that it undermined the voluntary nature of the alleged admissions made by him. *The People (at the suit of the Director of Public Prosecutions) v Paul Ward*, unreported, Court of Criminal Appeal, March 22, 2002.

Key Principle: Where a confession is obtained as a result of a deliberate and conscious breach of a constitutional right, the trial judge must exclude the evidence as inadmissible.

DPP v Madden [1977]

Madden was detained for questioning under s.30 of the Offences Against the State Act of 1939, but his detention continued for a period in excess of the period allowed by the Act. He had confessed during the unlawful period of detention. He was convicted after a trial before a jury. Madden appealed his conviction as the case for the prosecution was based squarely on his confession.

Held: The Court of Criminal Appeal held that the confession was inadmissible as there had been a deliberate and conscious breach of his constitutional rights, namely his right to liberty under Art.40.4.1 of the Constitution. *The People (at the suit of the Director of Public Prosecutions) v Madden* [1977] I.R. 336.

DPP v Healy [1990]

Paul Healy was arrested and detained on suspicion of being in unlawful possession of firearms. He was questioned about an attempted armed robbery and, in response to that questioning, he made a written confession. Shortly thereafter, a solicitor arrived at the station and asked to consult with Healy. This request was refused until the confession was written and complete. The Garda in charge stated that he thought it would be "bad manners" to interrupt the questioning.

Healy was subsequently charged with attempted murder, shooting with intent to cause grievous bodily harm and robbery, and the matter was sent to trial at the Central Criminal Court. The basis of the prosecution's case was the written confession. The Court ruled that Healy had been denied, without any excuse, his right of access to his solicitor and that the Court could not be satisfied that the incriminating admissions contained in his statement were made prior to the denial of that right. Accordingly, he directed the jury to enter verdicts of not guilty.

The Director of Public Prosecution appealed this verdict.

Held: The Supreme Court held that the right of an accused to reasonable access to his solicitor was derived from, and protected by, the Constitution and was not merely legal in origin. Healy should have been immediately informed of his solicitor's arrival and should have been given immediate access to him if requested. Where this right was deliberately and consciously breached by a member of the Garda Síochána, any admission subsequently obtained from a person detained in custody was inadmissible in evidence.

The Supreme Court held further that, in relation to the phrase "deliberate and conscious", the test was whether the actions of the Gardaí had been deliberate and conscious; the motives of the Gardaí were irrelevant and, in particular, it was immaterial whether they were aware that the refusal of access amounted to a breach of the defendant's constitutional rights. *The People (at the suit of the Director of Public Prosecutions) v Paul Healy* [1990] 2 I.R. 73.

Key Principle: The accused has a right of reasonable access to a lawyer.

DPP v Buck [2002]

Section 5(1) of the Criminal Justice Act of 1984 says that when a person is detained, the Station Commander shall inform that person of his right to consult a lawyer and if requested, shall cause the solicitor to be notified as soon as practicable. However, s.7(3) of that same Act says that a failure by a member of the Gardaí to observe any provisions of the Act "shall not of itself ... affect the lawfulness of the custody of the detained person or the admissibility in evidence of any statement made by him".

Anthony Buck was arrested on suspicion of murder and robbery. At the time of his arrest, he asked for a specific solicitor but it proved impossible to contact this solicitor. The same was true for Buck's second choice. Finally, a solicitor did arrive at the station to talk to Buck. After he had consulted with the solicitor, Buck made a written confession. Buck admitted that he had supplied the deceased with cannabis. When meeting with the deceased to supply him with the drug, it became clear that the deceased was carrying a large amount of money and, in his confession, Buck described how he and two others had murdered the deceased by repeatedly dropping a rock on his chest and thereafter stealing the money.

The solicitor testified at the trial that Buck knew he did not have to make a statement.

Buck argued that the Gardaí should have had regard to the difficulties they were likely to encounter in providing him with a solicitor when deciding when to arrest him, and that the subsequent denial of access to a solicitor amounted to a breach of his constitutional rights which made his detention unlawful. The unlawfulness of his detention meant that his confession was inadmissible, despite the fact that the confession was made after his consultation with the solicitor.

Buck further argued that the Criminal Justice Act 1984 (Treatment of Persons in Custody in Garda Síochána Stations) Regulations 1987, had been breached because reg.12(6) required the Gardaí to wait for a "reasonable time" to elapse after a solicitor has been requested before looking for a written statement in relation to the offence. The prosecution argued in return that even if such questioning did amount to a breach of Buck's constitutional rights, there had been no causal link between the questioning and the making of the confession as that had not been made until after Buck had received a visit from a solicitor.

The trial judge admitted the confession and Buck was convicted of murder and robbery, which was confirmed by the Court of Criminal Appeal. The Court of Criminal Appeal referred the matter to the Supreme Court as involving a point of law of exceptional public importance.

Held: The Supreme Court held that there were three propositions firmly established in our law with respect to admissibility in evidence of confessions, which were:

1. a confession, whether made to a police officer or any other person, would not be admitted in evidence unless it was proved beyond reasonable doubt to have been voluntarily made;

2. even where voluntarily made, a trial judge retained a residual discretion to exclude such a statement where it was made to a police officer otherwise than in accordance with certain

procedures, accepted in Ireland as being embodied in the English Judges' Rules, and

3. a statement would also be excluded where it had been obtained as the result of a conscious and deliberate violation of the accused's constitutional rights.

On the facts, the Supreme Court held that where a person is questioned after requesting a solicitor, but before the solicitor arrives, it could not be said that the constitutional right of access to a solicitor had necessarily been denied. However, a person's detention (in terms of a statute) was permissible only where his constitutional right of access to a solicitor was observed, and therefore his detention would become unlawful as soon as that right had been denied. Where the detained person had requested to see a solicitor and the Gardaí had made *bona fide* attempts to comply with that request, the admissibility of any statement made by the accused before the arrival of the solicitor must be decided by the trial judge as a discretionary matter based on principles of fairness to the detained person and to public policy.

Buck's appeal was dismissed and his conviction confirmed. *The People (at the suit of the Director of Public Prosecutions) v Anthony Buck* [2002] 2 I.R. 268.

Lavery v Member in Charge, Carrickmacross Garda Station [1999]

Deaglan Lavery was arrested under s.30 of the Offences Against the State Act of 1939, on suspicion that he had stolen the vehicle which was subsequently used to plant the bomb in the Omagh bombing. He was detained and questioned at Carrickmacross Garda Station but the interviews were not audio-visually recorded. Lavery's solicitor requested that he be allowed to be present during the interviews, or that complete notes of any interview held with his client be taken and made available to him, in order that he might properly advise his client, given that the statute in question allowed inferences to be drawn from a failure of a suspect to answer questions put to him. The solicitor argued that he needed to know what questions had been asked of his client, so that he could properly advise his client on his responses to those questions. These requests were refused by the superintendent in charge of the investigation.

The matter was brought before the District Court where an application was made to extend the period of detention for a further 24 hours. At this hearing, Lavery's solicitor repeated his request that he be allowed to see the notes of the interviews. The superintendent claimed privilege over these notes, and the District Court judge upheld the submission of privilege.

Lavery applied to the High Court for his immediate release. His argument was that the legislation required that his solicitor should be given access to the documents that he had requested and, once this request was refused, his detention became unlawful and he should be released. The High Court accepted this argument and ordered Lavery's release.

The respondent appealed to the Supreme Court.

Held: The Supreme Court found that while no privilege could be claimed by the State over the interview notes, its refusal to make those notes available to Lavery's solicitor did not render his detention unlawful. The detained person was not entitled to "regular updates and running accounts of the progress of their investigations". The solicitor was not entitled to be present during the interviews, and there was no suggestion that the solicitor had been refused reasonable access to his client. However, if the detained person is subsequently charged with an offence, then he and his solicitor would be entitled to all relevant documentation. The appeal was successful and the decision of the High Court was overturned. *Deaglan Lavery v the Member in Charge, Carrickmacross Garda Station* [1999] 2 I.R. 390.

Commentary

These decisions of the Supreme Court are in stark contrast to the well-known American decision of *Miranda v Arizona* (384 U.S. 436 (1966)), particularly concerning the ruling that, in Ireland, a detained suspect does not have the right to have a solicitor present throughout any questioning. It has been standard practice in America for decades that a suspect has the right to have his lawyer present when questioned.

THE JUDGES' RULES

The Judges' Rules have been inherited from the English and are a list of directions for the police when obtaining statements from people in custody. Although these Rules are administrative directions and do not have the force of statute, good reasons will need to be supplied before the courts will accept a breach of, or departure from, these Rules. Therefore, although a confession obtained in breach of the Rules is not automatically inadmissible, the trial judge will need to be convinced that the breach of the Rules was not of such a nature as to cause the confession to be inadmissible.

These Rules can be summarised as follows:

1. When a police officer is endeavouring to discover the author of a crime, there is no objection to his putting questions in respect thereof to any person or persons, whether suspected or not, from whom he thinks that useful information may be obtained.

2. Whenever a police officer has made up his mind to charge a person with a crime, he should first caution such person before asking him any questions, or any further questions as the case may be.

3. Persons in custody should not be questioned without the usual caution being first administered.

4. If the prisoner wishes to volunteer any statement, the usual caution should be administered. It is desirable that the last two words of such caution should be omitted, and that the caution should end with the words "be given in evidence".

5. The caution to be administered to a prisoner should, therefore, be in the following words: "Do you wish to say anything in answer to the charge? You are not obliged to say anything unless you wish to do so, but whatever you say will be taken down in writing and may be given in evidence." Care should be taken to avoid the suggestion that his answers can only be used in evidence *against* him, as this may prevent an innocent person from making a statement which might assist to clear him of the charge.

6. A statement made by a prisoner before there is time to caution is not rendered inadmissible in evidence merely because no caution has been given, but in such a case he should be cautioned as soon as possible.

7. A prisoner making a voluntary statement must not be

cross-examined, and no question should be put to him about it except for the purpose of removing ambiguity in what he has actually said. For instance, if he has mentioned an hour without saying whether it was morning or evening, or has given a day of the week and day of the month which do not agree, or has not made it clear to what individual or what place he intended to refer in some part of his statement, he may be questioned sufficiently to clear up the point.

8. When two or more persons are charged with the same offence and their statements are taken separately, the police should not read these statements to the other persons charged, but each of such persons should be given by the police a copy of such statements and nothing should be said or done by the police to invite a reply. If the person charged desires to make a statement in reply, the usual caution should be administered.

9. Any statement made in accordance with the above rules should, whenever possible, be taken down in writing and signed by the person making it after it has been read to him and he has been invited to make any corrections he may wish.

DPP v Farrell [1978]

George Farrell was charged and convicted of placing and exploding a bomb in Mill Street, Pettigo, County Donegal, on September 28, 1973. He was sentenced to 15 years' imprisonment.

Farrell appealed his conviction. The grounds of his appeal were that he had been detained in excess of the 24 hours allowed by s.30 of the Offences Against the State Act, that anything said after that period of 24 hours had occurred during an unlawful detention and was, therefore, inadmissible, and that at the time of his detention, he was not informed of his right to consult with a solicitor and that he had a constitutional right to have a medical examination at the beginning of his detention.

One of the provisions relied on by Farrell was Rule 9 of the Judges' Rules.

Held: None of the provisions relied on by Farrell was authority for the submission that a suspect who is detained under s.30 of the Act of 1939 has a constitutional right to the services of a solicitor and a doctor before being questioned by the police. The second 24 hours of Farrell's detention was unlawful in that it had not been authorised in the proper manner. Despite this, as Rule 9 of the Judges' Rules did not have the force of law, it was within the discretion of the trial judge to consider whether or not to allow evidence of an incriminatory oral statement made voluntarily by the detained person. In this case it had not been shown that the trial judge had exercised his discretion improperly in allowing this evidence.

The appeal was allowed, however, as the second period of detention was unlawful and therefore all the evidence given during that period was inadmissible. *The People (at the suit of the Director of Public Prosecutions) v George Samuel Farrell* [1978] I.R. 13.

Key Principle: Any breach of the Judges' Rules can be cured by a subsequent compliance with the Rules.

DPP v Buckley [1990]

Nicholas Buckley was arrested for armed robbery and detained in terms of s.30 of the Offences Against the State Act of 1939. During his first interrogation a statement made by a co-accused was read to him and his verbal response to that statement was noted. During his second interrogation the co-accused was brought into the room and their conversation was recorded. A third interrogation followed where Buckley was given the required cautions and thereafter he made a confession.

At the trial, the trial judge held that the statement made in the first interrogation was inadmissible as it was in violation of Rule 8 of the Judges' Rules. The statement made during the second interrogation was inadmissible as the entry of the co-accused was a *novus actus* and Buckley should have been newly cautioned. However, the confession made during the third interrogation was ruled admissible and Buckley was convicted on the basis of that confession.

Buckley appealed his conviction. He argued that having previously made incriminating statements in circumstances that rendered them inadmissible, he no longer had a free will by the time of the third interrogation and, therefore, the trial judge should have excluded the confession made at that third interrogation.

Held: The Court of Criminal Appeal held that where a statement is excluded because it was obtained in breach of the Judges' Rules, but where there is no question of threat, promise or oppression, subsequent statements made by that person following caution are not tainted by the circumstances of the original breach, and are therefore admissible.

The appeal was dismissed and the conviction was confirmed. *The People (at the suit of the Director of Public Prosecutions) v Nicholas Buckley* [1990] 1 I.R. 14.

THE REGULATIONS IN TERMS OF THE CRIMINAL JUSTICE ACT

The Criminal Justice Act (Treatment of Persons in Custody in Garda Síochána Stations) Regulations of 1987 set out rules which should be followed by the Gardaí when they are arresting, detaining or interrogating someone.

These Regulations are quite lengthy but the following articles are the ones that seem to have attracted the most scrutiny from the courts:

- Article 6 says that a custody record must be kept by the member in charge of the Garda station for every person who is in custody, with details about the person's detention, *e.g.* when they were detained, when they were interviewed and who interviewed them.

- Article 8 says that the member in charge should inform an arrested person of his right to consult a solicitor.

- Article 12 regulates the conduct of interviews. They must be conducted in a fair and humane manner. No more than two Gardaí should question an arrested person at any one time and no more than four Gardaí should be present during an interview. Interviews should be no longer than four hours before a break must be taken, irrespective of whether the accused person wishes to continue. Where an arrested person asks for a solicitor, a reasonable period of time must be allowed to pass without the arrival of the solicitor before that person is asked to make a written statement. An arrested person should not be questioned between midnight and 8.00 a.m. except with the authority of a member in charge, and this authority should not be granted unless (1) the arrested person has been taken to the station during that time; or (2) the person is detained under s.4 of the 1984 Act, and has not consented in writing to the suspension of questioning; or (3) the member in charge has reasonable grounds for believing that to delay in questioning would involve a risk of injury to persons or serious loss of, or damage to, property. Article 12 also instructs the Gardaí to keep a record of interviews with arrested persons—there would need to be compelling reasons why there was not an audio or an audio-visual recording of an interview.

• Article 13 concerns minors and stipulates that an accused or arrested person under the age of 17 (or a person reasonably believed to be under the age of 17) should have a parent or guardian present before being questioned or asked to make a statement. Again, the member in charge has the authority to allow questioning to take place without a parent or guardian but this authority shall not be given unless (1) it has not been possible to communicate with a parent or guardian; (2) one has not attended within a reasonable period of time; (3) it is not practical for one to attend within a reasonable period of time; or (4) the member in charge has reasonable grounds for believing that to delay questioning the person would involve a risk of injury to persons, serious loss of, or damage to, property, destruction of or interference with evidence, or the escape of accomplices.

DPP v McFadden [2003]

Gerry McFadden was arrested in Donegal on suspicion of driving a motor vehicle under the influence of alcohol. He was taken to the station, cautioned, and was asked to submit to a body search, which is standard practice to detect a concealed weapon. Article 17(1) of the Criminal Justice Act 1984 (Treatment of Persons in Custody in Garda Síochána Stations) Regulations 1987 provides that: "A member conducting a search of a person in custody shall ensure, so far as practicable, that the person understands the reason for the search and that it is conducted with due respect for the person being searched."

McFadden said that he had no objection to being searched. Whilst being searched, a wallet was found in his back pocket. McFadden became agitated and told the Gardaí not to "go near the wallet". The wallet was searched, ostensibly to establish his identity and address. The search of the wallet revealed a document containing the address, familial details, car and car registration number and church attendance of a superintendent in what was then the Royal Ulster Constabulary. McFadden was convicted on July 30, 2001 by the Special Criminal Court of being in possession of information of such a nature that it was likely to be useful in the commission of a serious offence by members of an unlawful organisation, contrary to s.8 of the Offences Against the State (Amendment) Act 1998. He was sentenced to four years' imprisonment. The trial court found that despite an inadequate explanation having been given by the Gardaí for the need to search the wallet, this was not serious enough to invalidate the search and render inadmissible the evidence of the document.

McFadden appealed his conviction to the Court of Criminal Appeal.

Held: The court found that although the initial body search was legal in that it was conducted with McFadden's consent, he never consented, and in fact objected, to any examination of the contents of his wallet or to the retention by the Gardaí of the document found therein. A member of the Garda Síochána cannot engage in such a procedure without the consent of the person whose person, property or effects are being searched unless authorised by law.

The lawful exercise of the power to search a person without their consent and to retain articles found thereby is subject to the precondition that a citizen is informed of the reason for the search. McFadden was at no stage told by the Gardaí why he was being searched or why the contents of his wallet were being examined or informed as to the power, if any, that the Gardaí were relying on to justify the search. This was in breach of Regulation 17(1) of the Criminal Justice Act 1984 (Treatment of Persons in Custody in Garda Síochána Stations) Regulations 1987 made under s.7 of the Criminal Justice Act 1984.

A breach of the fundamental requirement of the law that a police officer who is carrying out a search of a person without his consent informs that person of the legal justification for so interfering with his constitutional rights cannot be considered as of such little importance as to justify a departure from the regulation.

The appeal was upheld and McFadden's conviction was quashed. *The People (at the suit of the Director of Public Prosecutions) v Gerald Anthony McFadden* [2003] 2 I.L.R.M. 201.

DPP v Diver [2005]

John Diver was arrested and charged with his wife's murder. His wife, Geraldine, died in her motor car outside a builder's yard. Through the use of CCTV footage, the investigating officer was able to track her movements in the motor car until the time of her murder. The builder's yard was about three minutes' drive, and eleven minutes' walk, from the house where Diver and his wife lived. At 9.40 p.m. on the same evening, the video camera at the builder's yard showed the victim's car arriving at the entrance to the yard. At 9.55 p.m. all the lights in the car went off. At 10.01 p.m. a man, who it was not possible to identify on the film, got out of the car via the rear door on the driver's side. The body of Mrs Diver was later found in the car. She had been strangled. Diver told the investigating officer that he was caring for his children at the time of the murder—in effect, an alibi defence.

The prosecution led evidence that Diver had ample motive for murder. His wife was a lot younger than he, and their marriage had been in trouble for some time since his wife began having an open affair with a younger man, with whom she intended to have a child. She had also reversed a previous agreement with Diver that he would have custody of the children and the matrimonial home in the event of their separation.

Following his arrest, Diver was interviewed on five separate occasions at the Garda station by various officers, who recorded three of those interviews, not audio-visually, but in writing. Two of the interviews were completely unrecorded, one of them being an interview in which Diver had consistently denied any involvement in the crime. His two children also gave statements to the police regarding their father's movements on the night that their mother was murdered. At the trial, despite objections by the defence, the three recorded interviews and the children's statements were admitted in evidence. The children were questioned about their statements, but they denied the content of those statements, maintaining that the officer who had taken down their statements had done so incorrectly. The statements themselves were never produced in evidence, and the prosecution was refused permission to call the officer in question.

Clearly the testimony of the children regarding their father's movements on the night in question was crucial. In fact, their original accounts exonerated their father, as they said he had been in the house all evening except when he left to buy food at a nearby take-away. He returned with this, and realised he had forgotten noodles. He set out to get them but returned without them because, he said, it had started to rain. Both on deposition in the District Court (where they were called by the prosecution) and at the trial (where they were called by the defence) the children's timings were difficult to reconcile with Diver having time to get to the builder's yard and back between 9.40 and 10.01 p.m., (the time of the murder as shown on the video recording), particularly as he had to get the food as well. His daughter's testimony was very precise as she remembered the programme that she was watching on the television when Diver left and returned.

In addition, there was no evidence that Diver had any vehicle or bicycle available to him on the relevant night. However, an independent eyewitness testified that he had seen Diver in the back of his wife's car at the end of the RTÉ One News. The trial judge described this evidence as the most important evidence in the trial. This evidence was consistent with the evidence of a lorry driver who saw a woman in the driver's seat of a car parked outside the builder's yard with her arms down by her sides. He saw two hands "coming from behind her" and covering her breasts.

The jury was permitted to consider the accuracy and credibility of the children's evidence by reference to the alleged content of statements which had not been proved. The trial judge accepted that the Gardaí had been in breach of the relevant regulations for the treatment of persons in custody, but relied on s.7(3) of the Criminal Justice Act 1984, which says that the failure on the part of the Gardaí to observe the regulations should not affect the lawfulness of the custody of the person or the admissibility of any statement made by him.

Diver was convicted of murder and received a mandatory life sentence. His application for leave to appeal was dismissed by the

Court of Criminal Appeal, but that court did grant him a certificate allowing him to appeal to the Supreme Court in terms of s.29 of the Courts of Justice Act 1924.

The question to the Supreme Court was whether the trial judge was correct in exercising his discretion to admit the statements made by Diver as evidence.

Held: The Supreme Court held that it was not permissible to cross-examine on a document that had not been proved before the court.

The court held further that the failure by the trial judge to include in his ruling the words "of itself" in s.7(3) of the 1984 Act had resulted in a misdirection in law in a very significant way. It followed that the correct approach had not been taken to the issue of the admissibility of Diver's alleged statements in his interviews with the police. Further, since the children's statements had not been proved, the jury should not have been permitted to consider them for any purpose.

The conviction was quashed and the matter sent for retrial. *The Director of Public Prosecutions v John Diver* [2005] IESC 57.

Note: The retrial of John Diver was completed in the Central Criminal Court on July 12, 2006. He was acquitted.

CORROBORATION OF CONFESSIONS

Whilst not necessarily sufficient to have the confession immediately excluded, the fact that a confession is uncorroborated means that it must be treated with caution.

Key Principle: In terms of s.10(1) of the Criminal Procedure Act 1993, where the prosecution relies on the uncorroborated confession of the accused, that confession must be treated with caution.

DPP v Connolly [2003]

Martin Connolly was accused of breaking and entering, and stealing a video-recorder and a Playstation. The only evidence against him was a signed confession. One of the grounds of his appeal was that the trial judge had failed to give an adequate direction to the jury on the necessity of regarding the confession with caution, given that s.10(1) of the Criminal Procedure Act 1993 says the following:

> "(1) Where at the trial of a person on indictment evidence is given of a confession made by that person and that evidence is not corroborated, the judge shall advise the jury to have due regard to the absence of corroboration.
>
> It shall not be necessary for a judge to use any particular form of words under this section."

In relation to the weight to be given to the written confession, the judge directed the jury as follows:

> "Now it is a statement of admission made by [the accused] on the garda case and it is a statement that is unsupported by exterior evidence. There is no other piece of evidence, what is known as corroboration, tending to support it. No forensics were carried out. There was no other property or nothing else of a physical nature or otherwise tending to link the accused to the statement. That is something that you should bear in mind in applying your considerations to it."

Held: The Court of Criminal Appeal found that the phrase "due regard", as used in s.10 of the Criminal Procedure Act 1993, was intended to connote an objective and normative standard of attention to be paid to the absence of corroboration. The phrase was not self-explanatory and should be explained to the jury in terms of the meaning of corroboration and the factual nature of the prosecution's case. What was "due" in any particular case would vary and some attempt had to be made to suggest what the jury needed to look for in the absence of corroboration. In order to advise meaningfully that "due regard" be paid to the absence of corroboration, the term was to be properly, and not merely technically, explained.

The court continued that it might also be necessary to briefly and meaningfully explain why it was natural to look for corroboration in serious cases and why in some cases this did not always occur. Depending on the facts of the individual case, it might be a good idea to say something about why corroboration would be especially desirable in confession cases.

The court said that the phrase "something you should bear in mind", as used by the trial judge in his charge to the jury to advise on the issue of corroboration, was vague and less forceful than the statutory phrase "to have due regard".

Connolly's conviction was quashed and a re-trial ordered. *The People (at the suit of the Director of Public Prosecutions) v Martin Connolly* [2003] 2 I.R. 1.

10. Evidence Obtained in Violation of the Constitution

Evidence which is relevant to the issues before the court might still be declared inadmissible on policy grounds. For example, the court might decide that the probative value of the evidence is insufficient to justify the methods used to obtain such evidence.

This policy approach is grounded in three fundamental principles:

1. If the State was allowed to break the law in its efforts to bring criminals to justice, the legitimacy of the criminal justice system would be undermined.

2. The incentive for illegal conduct is removed if the State and its officers know that any evidence obtained illegally or unconstitutionally will be excluded.

3. The courts have the task of protecting the constitutional rights of the accused person, and must provide effective remedies if these rights are violated.

It would seem that the third principle is the foundation of the exclusionary rule in Irish law, as it is the one that the Supreme Court has most often endorsed.

Key Principle: The court must exclude evidence which has been obtained as a result of a deliberate and conscious violation of the constitutional rights of the accused and where no extraordinary excusing circumstances exist.

Commentary

The leading authority in this area is the Supreme Court decision in *People (A-G) v O'Brien* [1965] I.R. 142, which has been discussed in Chapter 1.

The phrase "a deliberate and conscious violation" is ambiguous. It might mean that the Gardaí must intend to breach the accused's constitutional rights, or it might mean that the act that caused the breach must be deliberate. The second approach should be the preferred approach as ignorance of the law should never be an excuse and the intention of the offending Gardaí should not, therefore, be a factor when deciding on the admissibility of the evidence. If the purpose of the exclusionary rule is to protect the accused by making illegal or unconstitutional evidence inadmissible, it is irrelevant to consider the motive of the person who procured the evidence.

Key Principle: For evidence to be excluded there must be:

- a breach of an accused's constitutional rights;
- a causative link between that breach and the evidence obtained; and
- no extraordinary excusing circumstances.

DPP v Kenny [1990]

Mark Kenny was convicted for trafficking in controlled drugs and sentenced to five years' imprisonment.

The evidence was that two members of An Garda Síochána were observing Kenny's house in Rathmines, Dublin, and observed what they thought was drug trafficking. Garda Conway radioed a colleague, requesting him to obtain a search warrant from a peace commissioner in terms of s.26(1) of the Misuse of Drugs Act.

The search warrant was issued based on the allegations made by Garda Conway, rather than upon any hard evidence before the Peace Commissioner to which he could apply his own mind. The Peace Commissioner (who died before Kenny's trial) did not make any further enquires in order to satisfy himself that there were reasonable grounds for the suspicions of the two officers.

Armed with the search warrant, the officers knocked on the door, and when their knocks were not answered, and knowing that Kenny was inside, they forced entry through a window and found Kenny in possession of controlled drugs, for which he took responsibility.

Kenny appealed his conviction to the Court of Criminal Appeal, arguing that the entry into his house with an invalid warrant was in violation of his constitutional rights. The Court of Criminal Appeal turned down his appeal, but sent the matter to the Supreme Court on a point of law of exceptional public importance.

Held: In a split decision of 3 to 2, the Supreme Court upheld the appeal and quashed Kenny's conviction. The Court confirmed that evidence obtained by an invasion of the personal rights of a citizen protected by the Constitution must be excluded in criminal proceedings unless there are extraordinary excusing circumstances justifying its inclusion.

The Court held further that where the breach was carried out consciously and deliberately, it is immaterial whether the person carrying out that act was aware that it was illegal or that it amounted to a breach of the accused's constitutional rights—the evidence must be excluded.

On the facts, the Court held that the Peace Commissioner had to be satisfied that there were reasonable grounds for the issue of a warrant, and this decision had to be an independent decision based on the facts before him. A failure to make this independent decision would be a failure to protect the inviolability of the dwelling under Art.40.5 of the Constitution. *The People (at the suit of the Director of Public Prosecutions) v Mark Kenny* [1990] I.L.R.M. 569.

Key Principle: Evidence might be admitted even where that evidence was in breach of the constitutional rights of the accused, but where the breach of those rights was necessary in order to protect or vindicate a competing or "superior" constitutional right.

DPP v Delaney [1997]

Michael Delaney was charged with using words with intent to provoke a breach of the peace, as were Wayne Kelly, Alan Lawless and David Crowley. Wayne Kelly, Alan Lawless, Anthony Lawless and David Crowley were also charged with producing an article capable of inflicting serious injury during the course of a dispute—in this case, a firearm. David Crowley was further charged with unlawfully assaulting Garda John Ferry in the due execution of his duty, as well as failing to answer to his bail.

Sergeant Nicholas McGrath gave evidence that he and nine other Gardaí went to the Liberties area in Dublin after a report of a disturbance. There was a large crowd in the street, some of whom were armed with sticks. They moved away on the arrival of the Gardaí. This crowd was hostile to the occupants of flat No.51, with some threatening to petrol-bomb and burn down the flat.

McGrath testified that he had looked in the window. Delaney and the others had barricaded themselves in. They were armed. McGrath asked them to come out and said they would be escorted away, but they refused and told him not to enter the flat.

McGrath testified that two women told him that there were children in the flat and so he entered the flat immediately, without a warrant, as he believed that he had to protect the children inside. All five accused persons were arrested in the flat. There was a woman with four children on a bed upstairs in the flat. She was the mother of Wayne Kelly, and the children were his siblings. They were unharmed.

The accused were convicted in the District Court. They appealed on the basis that the entry of the Gardaí into the flat was in violation of their constitutional rights to the inviolability of the dwelling. The High Court turned down the appeal and held that the Gardaí had been entitled to enter the dwelling forcibly. This decision was appealed to the Supreme Court.

Held: The Supreme Court turned down the appeal and confirmed the convictions. The Court pointed out that the only one who could assert any constitutional right in relation to a dwelling was Wayne Kelly, who was the occupier of the dwelling in question. The offences charged against him could be proved whether or not there was a breach of any constitutional provision. The Court held that in the present case there had not been any breach of the Constitution. The sergeant had to make a decision in an extremely fraught situation. He was entitled to make the decision he took provided he made it *bona fide* and there was no suggestion that he did otherwise. The safeguarding of life and limb must be more important than the inviolability of the dwelling of a citizen, especially when it is under attack. *DPP v Michael Delaney; Wayne Kelly; Alan Lawless; Anthony Lawless and; David Crowley* [1997] 3 I.R. 453.

Commentary
The Delaney decision is often cited in support of the proposition that the exclusionary rule will only apply to evidence obtained in breach of the accused's constitutional rights and, accordingly, where the rights of a third party are breached, this cannot help the accused. This seems to have been an *obiter*, however, and a more positive pronouncement on this topic would be welcome.

Concerning the principle of choosing a "superior" constitutional right, the Supreme Court came to a similar decision in *People v Shaw* [1982] I.R. 1 (discussed in Chapter 9) when it admitted confessions from the accused despite their continued illegal detention, on the grounds that the continued detention was in an attempt to save the lives of two young women.

Key Principle: There must be a direct causative link between the breach and the evidence obtained. In other words, the evidence sought to be excluded must have been obtained as a result of the breach of the accused's constitutional rights.

Walsh v District Justice O'Buachalla and the DPP [1991]

John Walsh was convicted of drunk driving (192 milligrams of alcohol per 100 millilitres of blood—92 milligrams over the permitted level). The evidence was that he had been arrested and brought to a Garda station, where he remained pending the arrival of a medical practitioner. He was given a document entitled "Information for Persons in Custody", which stated that arrested persons could communicate privately with a solicitor, either by telephone or at the station. Walsh did not bother to read the document, and only did so because the arresting officer insisted that he do so. Walsh had access to a telephone, but did not attempt to contact a solicitor. When the medical practitioner arrived about 40 minutes later, Walsh asked to see a solicitor. The arresting officer, Garda John Fahy, believed that this was a delaying tactic to avoid giving a specimen. He refused the request, informing Walsh that he could contact a solicitor as soon as the specimen had been taken. After the specimen was taken, Walsh did not try to contact a solicitor.

On review, Walsh argued that the specimen had been taken in breach of his constitutional right of access to a solicitor, and therefore should be inadmissible.

Held: The High Court held that evidence obtained following a deliberate and conscious breach of an accused person's constitutional rights must be excluded only if it had been obtained as a result of that breach. In the absence of a causative link between the breach and the obtaining of the evidence, such evidence was admissible.

The Court did not think that there had been any breach of any constitutional right, as Walsh had previously been given ample opportunity to contact a solicitor, but for the purposes of argument, even if it was assumed that there had been a breach of Walsh's constitutional rights, the specimen had been obtained after, but not as a result of, that breach. Walsh was obliged by statute to give a specimen of blood or urine and advice from a solicitor could not have altered that position. *John Walsh v District Justice Donnacha O'Buachalla and the Director of Public Prosecutions* [1991] 1 I.R. 56.

Key Principle: Where evidence is obtained as a result of a deliberate or a malicious breach of the constitutional rights of the accused, the court will not necessarily apply the causation requirement and might exclude evidence obtained after the breach occurs. This is similar to the "fruits of the poisonous tree" approach of American law.

Trimbole v Governor of Mountjoy Prison [1985]

Robert Trimbole, an Australian citizen, was arrested on suspicion of illegally possessing a firearm and ammunition. On application, the High Court ordered his release on the grounds that the arresting Garda did not have sufficient grounds for coming to a reasonable suspicion that Trimbole did have a firearm or ammunition.

Upon his release, Trimbole was re-arrested, this time with a view to extraditing him to Australia, where there were 18 warrants for his arrest, including some on charges of forging passports, armed robbery, heroin trafficking and murder.

It was clear that Trimbole's arrest in terms of the Offences Against the State Act was a deliberate attempt to hold him, and prevent him from leaving the country whilst the necessary extradition laws came into existence. Trimbole's counsel spoke of "kidnapping".

The High Court concluded that Trimbole's detention was a "gross misuse of the law" amounting to a "conscious and deliberate violation of constitutional rights". The High Court held further that there were no extraordinary excusing circumstances, and that Trimbole's custody was tainted by the illegality of his original arrest. The Court ordered that Trimbole be released immediately.

The Governor of Mountjoy Prison appealed.

Held: The Supreme Court dismissed the appeal and held that the courts not only have an inherent jurisdiction, but a positive duty, to protect persons against the invasion of their constitutional rights and, where invasion did occur, to restore as far as possible the person so damaged to the position in which he would be if his rights had not been invaded and to ensure as far as possible that persons acting on behalf of the Executive who consciously and deliberately violate the constitutional right of citizens do not benefit from that invasion. This principle of our law is of wider application than just the admissibility of evidence or the punishment of persons for contempt of court by unconstitutional action.

On the facts, the Supreme Court held that the illegality of Trimbole's arrest was not validated by subsequent lawful remand or detention orders. Whilst the charges against him in Australia were of the most serious kind, his guilt or innocence on those charges did not impact on his basic rights to fair procedures.

The Supreme Court did make it clear that the original unlawful arrest could not gain Trimbole any long-term or permanent immunity from extradition. *Robert Trimbole (Otherwise Known as Michael Hanbury) v the Governor of Mountjoy Prison* [1985] I.L.R.M. 465; *State (Trimbole) v the Governor of Mountjoy Prison* [1985] I.R. 550.

Commentary
It might be argued that Robert Trimbole was a very unsavoury character, and his extradition was clearly in the public interest. At the same time, the actions of the State in holding him unlawfully, whilst hurriedly passing the required extradition laws, was so gross a violation of the law that it could not be allowed under any circumstances. The Supreme Court made it clear that legal procedures had to be followed, even by the Executive.

Key Principle: If evidence is obtained in breach of an accused's constitutional right, it may still be admitted if there are extraordinary excusing circumstances in the case. The prosecution bears the burden of proving the existence of such circumstances.

Freeman v DPP [1996]

Freeman and two other men were unloading stolen goods from a van and carrying them into his house. The Gardaí had been tipped off, and were driving towards Freeman's house. When the thieves saw their car approaching, they ran into the house and slammed the door.

The Gardaí forcibly entered the house without waiting for a warrant. They discovered various stolen goods inside, namely cigarettes, alcohol, and two ornamental muskets. The thieves ran out the back door but were caught on the street and arrested.

A search warrant was obtained after the arrest and a pair of shoes was found that had been used in robbing the shop from which the stolen goods had been taken. A search of a van in the garden revealed five crates of beer, more cigarettes and cigars, and two ornamental horses' heads.

Freeman was convicted and appealed his conviction on the basis that the search and seizure by the Gardaí was in breach of his constitutional rights and, therefore, the discovery of the stolen goods and his subsequent arrest were illegal.

Held: The High Court accepted that the Gardaí had entered the house in breach of Freeman's constitutional right to the inviolability of his dwelling. However, the evidence of the stolen goods inside the house was admissible because there were extraordinary excusing circumstances. The men had been caught *in flagrante delicto* and the goods would have been destroyed by the time a warrant could have been obtained. *Freeman v Director of Public Prosecutions (At Suit of Garda Brunton)* [1996] 3 I.R. 565.

11. Expert and Opinion Evidence

As a general rule, witnesses can only testify about facts. It is the task of the jury, or the judge if there is no jury, to draw inferences from the facts presented in court, and witnesses must not be allowed to usurp this central function.

There are two notable exceptions to this general rule. First, expert witnesses may give opinion evidence; that is their primary function. Secondly, non-experts are sometimes allowed to give opinion evidence in defined circumstances, usually where their evidence would not make any sense if it were not accompanied by opinion.

Generally, a witness is considered an expert on the basis of their experience, training and knowledge. An expert witness is there to assist the court in coming to a conclusion in areas where the trial judge or jury might not have considerable expertise.

Key Principle: If the matter before the court or jury concerns something that does not require the testimony of an expert, then expert evidence is inadmissible.

DPP v Kehoe [1992]

Paul Kehoe and Sheila Murphy had a son together, but their relationship cooled somewhat thereafter. Pat Harvey, at the time a friend of Kehoe, began a relationship with Murphy, which caused Kehoe to become acutely jealous—so much so that he assaulted Harvey by striking him. Kehoe wrote a letter to Murphy saying that he wished to kill Harvey.

On March 1, 1990, Kehoe met Murphy in a pub. They had a few drinks and got on well together, so well that Murphy invited Kehoe back to her apartment. During the evening at Murphy's apartment, Kehoe decided to look in on his son. He entered the bedroom and found Pat Harvey there, asleep. Kehoe got a knife from the kitchen, ran back and stabbed Harvey to death.

Kehoe raised the defence of provocation. In support of this defence, a psychiatrist gave evidence about Kehoe's emotional state at the time of the killing. His evidence was to the effect that he had a great deal of experience with people who had been through emotional upset and he was, therefore, in a position to give a clinical pronouncement on the reality of Kehoe's defence.

Held: The psychiatrist could not give any relevant and admissible evidence in relation to the state of mind or temperament of Kehoe which Kehoe could not give himself. As to the question of whether Kehoe had the intention to kill and was telling the truth, these were matters entirely within the jury's function and a witness, no more than the trial judge or anybody else, is not entitled to trespass on the jury's function. *The People (at the suit of the Director of Public Prosecutions) v Paul Kehoe* [1992] I.L.R.M. 481.

Commentary
In addition to the principle clearly stated in *Kehoe*, namely that a witness is not allowed to usurp the function of the jury, the "ultimate issue" rule at common law says that an expert witness must not be allowed to give their opinion or draw inferences in respect of the "ultimate issue" (the crucial or determining aspect) in the case because this would usurp the function of the judge or jury. The rule is in decline as it does not make sense to say, on the one hand, that experts can testify on issues about which the judge or jury has no expertise, while, on the other hand, this expertise cannot be applied to the ultimate issue before the court.

Key Principle: The expert witness is called for his or her expertise and, as such, should regard themselves as "neutral" witnesses, there to help the court rather than to help one of the litigating parties.

National Justice Compania Naviera S.A. v Prudential Assurance Co. Ltd ("The Ikarian Reefer") [1993]

The plaintiff company were the owners of *Ikarian Reefer*, which was insured with the defendants. The vessel was insured against perils of the sea, fire and barratry. Under the policy, the vessel was valued at US$3m, of which 87.5 per cent was subscribed by the defendants.

On April 12, 1985 *Ikarian Reefer* ran aground on the shoals off Sherbro Island, Sierra Leone in the course of a voyage from Kiel to Abidjan. A fire broke out in the engine-room of the vessel and spread to the accommodation. The vessel was abandoned and the crew were rescued by a passing ship.

The dispute that had to be decided by the court was whether the defendants had shown that the fire was deliberately started by the captain and crew with the knowledge of the owners, the plaintiff. The court decided that the defendant had not proven that the fire was deliberately started.

A huge amount of evidence was given by expert witnesses for both sides, and this took up a lot of time in a very long trial. It was apparent that their evidence was contradictory and biased in favour of the party that called them. As a result of this, the court set out guidelines as to the duties and responsibilities of expert witnesses.

Held:

- Expert evidence presented to the Court should be, and should be seen to be, the independent product of the expert, uninfluenced as to form or content by the exigencies of litigation.

- An expert witness should provide independent assistance to the Court by way of objective, unbiased opinion in relation to matters within his expertise.

- An expert witness should state the facts or assumption upon which his opinion is based. He should not omit to consider material facts which could detract from his concluded opinion.

- An expert witness should make it clear when a particular question or issue falls outside his expertise.

- If an expert's opinion is not properly researched because he considers that insufficient data is available, then this must be stated with an indication that the opinion is no more than a provisional one.

- If, after exchange of reports, an expert witness changes his view on a material matter having read the other side's report or for any other reason, such change of view should be communicated to the other side.

National Justice Compania Naviera S.A. v Prudential Assurance Co. Ltd ("The Ikarian Reefer") [1993] 2 Lloyd's Rep. 68.

Key Principle: As a general rule, non-expert witnesses can give their opinion when it is so intertwined with the facts in their testimony that it is impossible to separate the facts from the opinion, or where it would not make any sense to state the facts without the opinion.

Evidence

Attorney-General v Kenny (1960)

Kenny was accused of driving a motor vehicle whilst under the influence of alcohol. The evidence of the arresting officer was that Kenny had appeared "bleary" and "smelling of drink". The Garda was thereafter allowed to express his opinion that Kenny was drunk at the time, and was further allowed to express his opinion as to how drunk Kenny was at the time.

Held: Drunkenness is a condition which is not so exceptional or so much outside the experience of the ordinary individual that it should require an expert to diagnose it. The judgment of Davitt P. in the High Court was confirmed by the Supreme Court. *Attorney-General (Ruddy) v Kenny* (1960) 94 I.L.T.R. 185.

Commentary

This question is largely academic in the modern age where prosecutions are based on breathalysers and, thereafter, blood-alcohol tests or urine-alcohol tests. The case might arise, however, where these tests are faulty in some respect, and the prosecution seeks to rely on the opinion of the arresting officer. There would be many non-expert witnesses who could give a considered and valid opinion on that topic, the obvious example being a Garda, who would probably see more drunk people than most.

An eyewitness is the other common exception to this rule, as they would describe conditions or visibility as "good" or "bad", someone's appearance as "friendly" or "menacing", a person's height as "tall" or "short", and so forth. These are opinions as they are descriptions which are relative, and formed by their own experience and belief, but which are not so out of the ordinary that one would need experts to draw inferences from the facts. In addition, eyewitness testimony would be worthless if the witness was not allowed to use subjective descriptions whilst testifying.

12. Privilege

INTRODUCTION

Privilege is a right which allows a witness to refuse to produce a document or to answer a question. Privilege only becomes an issue once a witness has been declared competent. Clearly, an incompetent witness has no need to claim privilege, as they will not be testifying in any event. Similarly, privilege does not mean that a witness can refuse to answer all questions or refuse to produce all documents. The privilege will relate to specific questions and to specific documents. The witness can still be forced to answer other questions, or to produce other documents. Marital privilege is the exception to this rule, and will be discussed later in this chapter.

Privilege is an obstacle to the truth and the foundation for most types of privilege is public policy, where the law regards the search for truth as being secondary to the potential harm that this search might cause to society.

To ensure a fair trial, all relevant evidence must be brought before the court. By excluding relevant matters, the doctrine of privilege restricts the right of a citizen to a fair trial and the administration of justice, and therefore requires constitutional justification.

There are two main types of privilege: public and private. Public privilege applies to the State, whilst private privilege applies to the individual.

PUBLIC PRIVILEGE

Public or public interest privilege is also referred to as State privilege or executive privilege and is linked to matters of state security or defence, although it could be extended to other instances of confidentiality.

Key Principle: Public privilege is based on the principle that the State must not be put in jeopardy by producing documents that may injure it.

Duncan v Cammell Laird & Co. Ltd [1941]

This matter arose from the *Thetis* Disaster. On June 1, 1939, the pride of the Royal Navy, the submarine *Thetis*, made its maiden dive. Conditions on board were extremely cramped, with the submarine carrying 103 men—twice the number she was designed to carry. Many were engineers from Cammell Laird, with only 69 of the 103 being sailors. Laird's workers were offered the opportunity to disembark prior to the dive, but all chose to stay. The initial attempt at a dive was unsuccessful, as the vessel, for some reason, was too light. The captain ordered that the torpedo tubes be flooded with seawater to add weight to the submarine. Without knowing that the outer torpedo doors were already open and the tubes full of seawater, the captain gave the order. The captain was also unaware that a few weeks earlier, a painter, working on the other side of the torpedo door, had allowed enamel to drip inside the test tap and solidify. With the test tap blocked, the captain believed it was safe to open the door inside the submarine. With hundreds of tons of water filling the first and second compartments, *Thetis* nose-dived. For three days, in the heart of Liverpool Bay, just 38 miles from land, the men on board battled the effects of carbon dioxide poisoning, waiting for a rescue which never came. The bodies of the men who suffocated remained inside *Thetis* for a further four months until the submarine was salvaged from the bottom of the bay.

The appellants were the families of these employees, and they were suing the employer, Cammell Laird, for damages. They sought discovery of the blueprints of the submarine, as this was necessary to pinpoint whether a design fault had been the primary cause of the tragedy. The First Lord of the Admiralty had made an affidavit in which he stated that such production would be contrary to the public interest. The appellants argued that the court should look behind the affidavit by examining the documents and thereafter decide whether the production of the blueprints would be contrary to the public interest, as claimed by the defendant.

Held: The court refused to go behind the affidavit of the First Lord of the Admiralty, and held that the affidavit was conclusive and binding on it, and, in such a case, the court should not order the production of the documents for its own inspection. The order for production was refused. *Duncan v Cammell Laird & Co. Ltd* [1941] 1 All E.R. 437.

Murphy v Dublin Corporation [1972]

Joseph Murphy wanted to develop certain of his lands, but the Council refused him planning permission. Shortly afterwards the Council made a compulsory purchase order of Murphy's land in terms of the Housing Act of 1966. The objections of Murphy and others led to a public inquiry by an inspector appointed by the Minister for Local Government. The inspector furnished a written report to the Minister. Murphy challenged the legality of the compulsory purchase order, and asked the Minister to disclose the report, but the Minister claimed that the production of the report would be contrary to public policy and the public interest.

Held: The Supreme Court held that it would not follow the *Duncan v Cammell Laird* decision as that decision was made in a country that did not have a Constitution, whereas in Ireland constitutional principles needed to be applied to the question. The essential conflict was between the duty of the State to administer justice and the duty of the State to exercise executive power and, as the Court was charged with the administration of justice, the document would have to be inspected by that Court before making a decision, and if the Court found that the document was relevant to the proceedings, the onus of establishing that the document should not be produced would fall on the party claiming the public privilege.

Joseph Murphy v the Right Honourable Lord Mayor, Aldermen and Burgesses of the County Borough of Dublin, and the Minister for Local Government [1972] I.R. 215.

Ambiorix Ltd v Minister for the Environment (No. 1) [1992]

The Minister for the Environment, in consultation with the Minister for Finance, declared a site belonging to Irish Life Assurance plc a "designated area" under s.6 of the Urban Renewal Act 1986. As a result of this decision, Irish Life stood to gain a lot of money and other economic benefits. The plaintiffs, who were property development companies, sought a declaration that the decision was *ultra vires* and contrary to the purposes of the Act of 1986 on the grounds that the decision was reached on inappropriate criteria or on a consideration of incorrect or insufficient material.

The High Court ordered discovery of relevant documents and memoranda. The Minister for the Environment appealed the order on the grounds of privilege in the public interest, based on the confidentiality of Cabinet communications, the disclosure of which could prejudice the collective responsibility of the Government. The Minister argued that the documents related to the formulation of policy and legislative proposals and belonged to a class of documents which were absolutely privileged and which did not require to be examined by the trial judge. The Minister also argued that a heavy onus of proof lay on the party seeking production of such documents to establish exceptional circumstances before the claim to privilege should be disallowed.

Held: The Supreme Court dismissed the appeal of the Minister and confirmed the principles formulated in the *Murphy* decision. The Supreme Court held that under the Constitution of Ireland, 1937, the administration of justice was committed solely to the courts and, therefore, any conflict between the public interest in the production of evidence and the public interest in the confidentiality of documents relating to the exercise of the executive power fell to be decided by the courts. The Executive could not prevent the courts from examining documents relevant to any issue in a civil trial for the purpose of deciding if they should be produced in evidence. The Court held that there was no obligation on the courts to examine any document and a claim of privilege could be upheld by the courts merely on the basis of a description of the nature or contents of a document. At the same time, no class of document was exempt from production by reason of the rank of the public servant creating it or the identity of the person for whom it was intended. Once a court was satisfied that a document was relevant, the onus of proof lay on the party claiming the privilege to show why it should not be produced in evidence.

The Supreme Court held further that any party to an action who obtained production of documents by discovery was prohibited from making use of those documents except for the purposes of that action and it was within the inherent jurisdiction of the courts to regulate the production of documents to prevent the infringement of this restriction. Consequently, those documents which constituted representations made by third parties to the government in the belief that such correspondence was confidential would be disclosed to the lawyers acting on behalf of the plaintiffs only, on the undertaking that they would not reveal their contents to their clients without the special leave of the trial court. *Ambiorix Ltd, Earlsfort Centre (Developments) Ltd, Ryde Developments (Ireland) Ltd and Sharnbrook Ltd v The Minister for the Environment, The Minister for Finance, Ireland, The Attorney-General and Irish Life Assurance plc* [1992] 1 I.R. 277.

Commentary

The court is being asked to perform a balancing act. The trial judge has to weigh up the public interest in the administration of justice—which favours disclosure—against the public interest being put forward in favour of non-disclosure. There could be any number of public interests put forward in favour of non-disclosure, and it is impossible to have a closed list. Some of the commonly encountered public interests considered by our courts are the public interest in the prevention and prosecution of crime (*Breathnach v Ireland (No.3)* [1993] 2 I.R. 458), the public interest in the security of the State (*Murphy v Dublin Corporation* [1972] I.R. 215), the public interest in the proper functioning of the public service (*Director of Consumer Affairs v Sugar Distributors Ltd* [1991] 1 I.R. 225), and the public interest in the maintenance of sound international relations (*Walker v Ireland* [1997] 1 I.L.R.M. 363).

What is important to remember is that it is the courts, and the courts alone, that make the decision whether a document is privileged or not.

Key Principle: Communications between members of the Garda Síochána are not necessarily protected by public interest privilege.

DPP v Holly [1984]

Michael Holly was charged with unlawful assault upon a Garda whilst trying to free his friend who had been arrested for drunk and disorderly conduct. The defence called upon the Garda, Michael Queally, who was allegedly the victim of the assault, to produce his original report about the incident. The prosecution argued that the report was protected by executive privilege and could not be produced.

Held: The High Court held that executive privilege cannot be claimed in respect of a class of document as such. The claim that communications between members of the Gardaí are inadmissible as evidence because, as a class, their admission would be against the public interest, was not acceptable. Since the State had not advanced specific grounds of possible damage to the public interest which might result from disclosure, the trial judge should have rejected the claim to privilege. If specific grounds had been advanced to the trial judge, it would have been necessary for the judge to read the document privately and determine its admissibility in accordance with the principles set out in the *Murphy v Dublin Corporation* decision. *The Director of Public Prosecutions (at the suit of Superintendent F. C. Hanley) v Michael Holly* [1984] I.L.R.M. 149.

PRIVATE PRIVILEGE

Private privilege is concerned with situations where a person acting in an individual capacity or in a private capacity (as opposed to acting as a public servant or in the service of the State) claims privilege. Accordingly, the concept of private privilege covers more diverse scenarios than those concerning public privilege.

Legal professional privilege

The efficiency and credibility of the judicial system relies on the notion that a client must be confident that what he or she tells the solicitor or barrister will stay with that solicitor or barrister and will go no further without the client's permission.

Key Principle: Legal professional privilege is more than a rule of evidence. It is a fundamental condition on which the administration of justice rests.

Miley v Flood **[2001]**

The Flood Tribunal was set up to investigate corruption within the planning system, with Justice Flood as the sole member.

Stephen Miley was the solicitor acting for a company that was under investigation by the Tribunal. He was summonsed to give evidence about the identity of parties who were suspected of being beneficial owners and/or principals of the company.

Miley appeared before the Tribunal but refused to furnish the information sought. He argued that he could not reveal these identities as the matter of client identity was covered by legal professional privilege and the parties in question had refused to waive this privilege.

His arguments were rejected by Judge Flood and he directed Miley to furnish the relevant information. Miley brought judicial review proceedings in the High Court seeking to quash the ruling.

Held: The High Court held that the information sought by the Tribunal was needed for preliminary investigations and Milcy's clients were not, therefore, entitled to the full protection of privilege, as they would have been had the matter involved a full legal action between parties.

The Court held that legal professional privilege was more than a mere rule of evidence. It was a fundamental condition on which the administration of justice as a whole rested. Privilege could not be claimed in respect of information passing for the purposes of securing legal assistance. Where it was established that a communication was made for the purpose of obtaining legal advice, that communication should be privileged except where waived by the client.

Confidentiality of information did not of itself create a privilege from disclosure. Moreover, Irish law did not recognise the concept of client identity privilege as the question of a client's identity was nothing more than a collateral fact and not relevant in general to the matter of the legal advice being sought. Even if it could be said to have been so recognised, it could only be recognised in circumstances where disclosure of such information would incriminate or reveal the actual advice given by the lawyer to the client. The onus would lie on the person seeking to uphold the claim of privilege to establish that their circumstances fell within such exception.

This judgment of the High Court was taken on appeal to the Supreme Court but the matter was thereafter settled and withdrawn before the Supreme Court could deal with it. *Stephen Miley v Judge Flood* [2001] 1 I.L.R.M. 489.

Legal advice privilege

There are two sub-categories of legal professional privilege: legal advice privilege and litigation privilege. As far as the first category is concerned, communications between a lawyer and a client for the purpose of giving or receiving legal advice are privileged. However, for a document or piece of information to be covered by legal advice privilege it must satisfy a number of requirements.

Key Principle: There must be a communication and that communication must be confidential.

Bord Na gCon v Murphy [1970]

Thomas Murphy was convicted of breaches of the Greyhound Industry Act 1958—failure to record a bet and pay the required levy on that bet. He appealed his conviction. The Board had written to Murphy, accusing him of contravening the Act and had asked him to respond. Murphy consulted with his solicitor and, thereafter, made a statement to his solicitor, setting out his side of the story and the solicitor replied to the Board, enclosing a written note of the statement. The Board wanted to lead the statement as evidence.

Held: Although the Supreme Court held that the statement was hearsay and therefore inadmissible, it did find the statement was not privileged because it was not intended that the contents would remain confidential, but that they would be disclosed to the Board. *Bord na gCon v Thomas Murphy* [1970] I.R. 301.

Key Principle: The communication must be made in the course of a professional legal relationship.

Buckley v Law Society [1994]

Thomas Buckley was injured in an accident at his workplace. He instructed a solicitor to act on his behalf. The solicitor accepted the work but took such a long time instituting proceedings for damages that Buckley's claim was out of time and was not allowed to go on (known as "statute barred").

Buckley sued the Law Society for allowing this solicitor to practise when its investigations should have revealed that the solicitor in question was not fit to practise. As it happened, the solicitor was subsequently struck off the roll of solicitors.

Buckley requested the Law Society to furnish him with copies of earlier complaints made against that particular solicitor. The Law Society refused to do so, claiming that these documents were privileged.

Held: The High Court rejected this claim of privilege, holding that there was no legal professional privilege in respect of any of the documents containing the complaints, as the people complaining about the conduct of the solicitor were not employing the Law Society as their solicitor. *Thomas Buckley v The Incorporated Law Society of Ireland* [1994] 2 I.R. 44.

Key Principle: The communication must be for the purpose of obtaining legal advice.

Smurfit Paribas Bank Ltd v AIB Finance Ltd [1990]

Smurfit Bank and AIB agreed to lend substantial amounts of money to the same third party. The third party arranged with both banks to put up assets as security for the respective loans. A dispute arose between the banks concerning an agreement reached between them concerning the service of the debt of this third party.

When proceedings were instituted, Smurfit Bank applied for an order directing AIB to make further and better discovery of all correspondence and instructions passing between AIB and the solicitors then acting for it in relation to a charge taken by AIB over the assets of the third party. AIB confirmed the existence of these documents but claimed privilege as they were either written by the solicitors acting for AIB at the time of the agreement with the third party and addressed to the defendant or vice versa.

Smurfit Bank argued that not all communications between solicitor and client were privileged, particularly when litigation was neither in existence nor contemplated.

The High Court agreed, and held that the documents were not privileged as they did not request or contain any legal advice and contained no information or remarks that could be regarded as confidential, being merely statements of fact concerning the transaction with the third party.

AIB appealed this finding to the Supreme Court.

Held: The Supreme Court confirmed the fundamental principle established in *Murphy v Dublin Corporation*, namely that the rights of a litigating party to privilege was a matter to be decided by the courts alone, which for this purpose had the power to examine the documents in question and also had to decide which was the superior interest in the circumstances of the particular case.

The Court held that the privilege might be extended further than instances of actual or contemplated litigation to cases of legal assistance other than advice, but for this extension to be justified the party claiming such an extension of the privilege needed to show that the documents in question were closely and proximately linked to the conduct of litigation. On the other hand, it was not desirable to extend the privilege to communications made to a lawyer for the purpose of obtaining legal assistance other than advice and which did not contain any relationship with the area of potential litigation.

The appeal was dismissed as in this case the legal assistance was of a nature other than legal advice, and accordingly did not deserve the protection of privilege. *Smurfit Paribas Bank Ltd v A.I.B. Finance Ltd* [1990] 1 I.R. 469.

Litigation privilege

Litigation privilege also refers to communications but here the net of privilege is spread slightly wider, protecting not only communications between solicitor and client, but also communications between a third party and the solicitor or client. Once again, however, in order to claim this privilege, a number of conditions must be satisfied.

Key Principle: Litigation must be pending or contemplated when the document is prepared or the communication made. A document will only be protected by litigation privilege if it was prepared for the dominant purpose of the pending or contemplated litigation.

Gallagher v Stanley [1998]

Avril Gallagher's son was born by caesarean section at the National Maternity Hospital after a long and difficult labour. The child was severely injured and disabled. Mrs Gallagher claimed that these injuries and disabilities were as a result of the negligence of the hospital staff responsible for the birth and sued the hospital for damages.

Discovery of documents was made in the usual fashion but the hospital claimed privilege in respect of statements made by three nurses who were on duty in the hospital at the relevant time, claiming that these statements had been made in contemplation of litigation. The hospital argued that the statements were not ordinary medical or treatment records, as they were made at the request of the matron when it became "apparent that the infant plaintiff had undergone an extremely difficult birth and that there was a substantial risk that he would suffer very serious injuries as a result thereof. The statements were made on a confidential basis in order to provide the legal advisors of the hospital with necessary material to advise in the event of a claim subsequently being made by, or on behalf of, the infant plaintiff."

In a supplementary affidavit the matron explained how, whilst she was on duty, Mr Gallagher had arrived at the hospital in a very angry state, complaining about the treatment of his wife, and soon thereafter one of the three nurses in question had informed her that the birth had been a very difficult one and that there was a distinct possibility that the baby had suffered serious injury. It was on that basis that she had requested the three nurses to prepare statements. She said that she had intended to supply these statements to the legal secretary of the hospital, and she had subsequently done so. She could even recall saying to the three nurses something along the lines of "the unfortunate birth of the child could result in litigation".

The High Court disallowed the claim of privilege, finding that the suggestion that the statements had come into existence in anticipation of proceedings was "unwarrantedly premature". The hospital authorities appealed this decision.

Held: The Supreme Court confirmed the finding of the High Court and dismissed the appeal. The Court held that it was essential that litigation should be "reasonably apprehended" at the least before a claim of privilege can be upheld. Whilst our society has become so litigious that the matron might have had grounds for thinking that litigation would follow the birth of the infant, the dominant purpose for which the documents in question came into being was not in anticipation of litigation. Her main concern when she asked for the statements was the recognition that she needed to be in a position to account for how the hospital and, in particular, her section, was run, and how the staff under her control had conducted themselves in this time of crisis. The court pointed out that if the hospital had prepared the statements solely in contemplation of litigation, they would at least have reduced them to affidavits. It was clear that these statements were primarily for the purposes of reviewing the procedures involved in the birth of the child. *Avril Gallagher (o.b.o. Infant Gallagher) v Dr Stanley and others* [1998] 2 I.R. 267.

Setting aside the privilege

The courts have recognised that there are certain situations where the demands of public interest outweigh the need for legal professional privilege.

Key Principle: Legal professional privilege will not protect communications in furtherance of a crime or a fraud, or communications in furtherance of conduct which is injurious to the interests of justice.

Attorney-General v Coleman [1945]

William Coleman was convicted of two counts of criminal abortion and was sentenced to a total of 15 years' imprisonment. He appealed his conviction to the Court of Criminal Appeal. One of his many grounds of appeal was the refusal by the trial judge to declare a certain document to be privileged and inadmissible as evidence against the accused.

The evidence showed that this document was written by Coleman and was in his possession when he was in Mountjoy Prison on remand and awaiting his trial. During a visit from his wife, the document fell on the ground, was picked up by a warder, and was eventually handed over to the Governor of the prison.

Coleman argued that the document was privileged as it had been written by him to be given to his solicitor. The trial judge examined the document and decided that it was a list of witnesses (other women on whom Coleman had committed abortions) that Coleman wanted to subornate. On that basis, the trial judge held that this was an exception to the legal professional privilege covering communications between client and solicitor.

Held: The Court of Criminal Appeal held that on a reading of the document in question, it could not reasonably bear any other meaning than an attempt to subornate witnesses. That being so, even if it had reached the solicitor, it would not be a privileged communication as it contemplated and suggested the commission of a crime. *The People (at the suit of the Attorney-General) v William Henry Coleman* [1945] I.R. 237.

Murphy v Kirwan [1993]

Patrick Murphy sought specific performance of an alleged agreement that he claimed to have with Anthony Kirwan. Kirwan counter-claimed for damages on the grounds that Murphy's claim was frivolous, vexatious and was taken to prevent him from performing another agreement. Murphy's case was dismissed and Kirwan's counter-claim was adjourned.

Kirwan then sought discovery of the legal advice received by Murphy in relation to the specific performance claim. Murphy argued that in the absence of an allegation of fraud this advice was privileged. The High Court rejected this argument and ordered Murphy to produce the documents in question. Murphy appealed this finding to the Supreme Court, arguing that professional privilege could only be defeated where it was used for purposes of fraud.

Held: The Supreme Court held that professional privilege cannot be claimed by persons who are guilty of conduct of moral turpitude or of dishonest conduct even though it may not be fraud. Nothing could be more injurious to the administration of justice than a malicious action which was an abuse of the legal process for an ulterior or improper purpose. The ruling of the High Court was confirmed, the appeal was dismissed, and Murphy was ordered to produce the documents. *Patrick Murphy v Anthony M.D. Kirwan* [1993] 3 I.R. 501.

Bula Ltd v Crowley (No.2) [1994]

Crowley was the Receiver of Bula Limited. Bula claimed that he had been negligent in failing to follow some legal advice he had obtained. They sought discovery of documents containing this legal advice. The High Court refused their application, holding that the documents contained legal advice and were, therefore, privileged. Bula appealed to the Supreme Court, arguing that Crowley's negligence justified the lifting of the privilege.

Held: The Supreme Court turned down the appeal and held that the documents were privileged. The exception to the doctrine of legal professional privilege was restricted to cases where allegations of fraud, criminal conduct or conduct constituting an interference with the administration of justice were made. All of these allegations contain a clear element of moral turpitude. Here, the plaintiffs were only claiming that the defendant was negligent. *Bula Limited (In receivership) and others v Laurence Crowley and others (No. 2)* [1994] 2 I.R. 54.

Crawford v Treacy [1999]

Treacy claimed to be the legal wife of the deceased and therefore entitled to at least part of his deceased estate. She was described as his wife by the testator in his will.

The evidence before the court was that they were married on August 19, 1958, in the Church of Ireland. The following year Treacy procured a church annulment, left the deceased, and settled in England. She was divorced from him in England on August 7, 1963. On August 27, 1963 she married in England but was divorced some 11 years later. In 1975 she returned to Ireland and recommenced living with the testator as his wife.

On November 5, 1981, Treacy and the testator entered into a separation agreement, in which they expressly recited that they had received advice that they remained always married and in which they each resigned their legal rights under Part IX of the Succession Act 1965. For the next nine years or so Treacy was in regular contact with the testator and in 1990 again resumed cohabitation with him as his wife. They lived together in a new house bought by the testator in 1990 and were living together when he died in 1996. The testator left a sum of £50,000 "to my wife". However, the value of the estate was in excess of £9 million. If Treacy could show that she was indeed the testator's wife, she would be entitled to a far greater amount than the legacy she had received.

Crawford claimed privilege over documents relating to the preparation of the last Will and Testament dated January 25, 1995. He argued that the documents were prepared in contemplation of proceedings as the testator envisaged at the time he was making his Will that Treacy would seek to assert entitlements as a spouse pursuant to the provisions of Part IX of the Succession Act 1965. Crawford further argued that the claim of privilege rested not only upon the basis of documents brought into existence in contemplation of litigation, but also upon the basis that it was legal professional advice obtained, although not necessarily in contemplation of litigation.

Treacy argued that if privilege did extend to these documents, then they fell within a recognised exception that this was not an action *inter partes* but was rather a quest for the testator's true intention. She also argued that the documents were not entitled to the protection of privilege as they were brought into existence in order to defeat her legal right, and were therefore tainted with moral turpitude.

Held: The documents sought by Treacy related to legal advice. There was nothing in the documents to suggest that there was any intent to set aside her legal entitlement. *Re Treacy (Deceased); Crawford and another v Treacy and others* [1999] 2 I.R. 171.

Key Principle: Legal professional privilege might not protect communications that help an accused person establish his innocence. This is a controversial notion and has not been decided by the Irish courts. The English courts have faced this issue, but the extent of the exception is still unclear.

R. v Barton [1972]

William Henry Barton was a legal executive at a firm of solicitors and was charged with fraudulent conversion, theft and falsification of accounts alleged to have been committed in the course of his employment. He subpoenaed a number of documents held by the solicitors as he claimed that these would show that he was innocent of the charges. The solicitors opposed his application on the ground that the documents in question were subject to legal professional privilege.

Held: There was no precedent to assist the court in this matter. Assuming that the documents in question were indeed protected by privilege, then on the basis of the rules of natural justice (as opposed to any cited authority), if there are documents in the possession or control of a solicitor which, on production, help to further the defence of an accused man, then no privilege attaches. *R. v William Henry Barton* [1972] 2 All E.R. 1192; [1973] 1 W.L.R. 115; 136 J.P. 614.

R. v Derby Magistrates' Court, Ex p. B [1996]

The appellant (a minor at the time) was arrested on suspicion of murdering a 16-year-old girl. The next day he confessed to the murder and was charged. In October, just before the beginning of his trial, he made a statement alleging that he and his stepfather had been present when the girl was killed, that his stepfather had carried out the murder and that he had assisted under duress. At his trial in November he was acquitted, but when subsequently interviewed by the police he stated that he alone had killed the girl. He later retracted that statement and made a further statement that his stepfather had carried out the murder.

In 1992 the stepfather was arrested and charged with the murder of the girl. At the stepfather's committal proceedings the appellant was called as a witness by the Crown. Counsel for the stepfather attempted to cross-examine him about instructions he had given to his solicitors in 1978 between his initial confession that he alone was responsible and his subsequent statement implicating his stepfather because the instructions were clearly inconsistent with the subsequent statement implicating his stepfather. When the appellant declined to waive his privilege, counsel for the stepfather applied to the magistrate conducting the committal proceedings for witness summonses directed to the appellant and his solicitor, requiring them to produce all attendance notes and proofs of evidence containing the instructions of the appellant to his legal advisers, but excluding the advice that they in turn had given him. The magistrate issued the summonses as requested. The appellant took the decision of the magistrate on review, but failed. The appellant appealed to the House of Lords.

Held: The House of Lords upheld the appeal. The court held that the appellant had been entitled to assert his privilege, with the result that the instructions given to his solicitors were inadmissible. The privilege was of an absolute and permanent nature and, therefore, the communications between a solicitor or counsel and a client seeking professional legal advice were immune from production. Legal professional privilege was not just an ordinary rule of evidence but a fundamental condition on which the administration of justice as a whole rested, since it was based on the principle that a client should be able to consult his lawyer in confidence and without fear that his communications would be revealed without his consent, because otherwise he might hold back half the truth. *R. v Barton* overruled. *R. v Derby Magistrates' Court, ex parte B* [1996] 1 A.C. 487; [1995] 4 All E.R. 526; [1995]; 3 W.L.R. 681.

Commentary
Should such a question come before an Irish court, it would need to be answered in terms of constitutional principles. The conflict would be between the right of a citizen to a fair trial, and the right of another citizen to confide in his solicitor or barrister in the knowledge that those confidences will never be revealed without his consent, which is regarded as essential for the proper administration of justice. It is futile to attempt to predict an outcome to this conflict between two constitutional rights, as Irish law is sufficiently flexible to allow courts to consider questions like this on a case-by-case basis.

Loss of privilege

There are situations where the courts will hold that legal professional privilege has been lost and cannot be claimed by the witness. In other words, the legal professional privilege was originally in place, but due to the actions of the person entitled to the privilege, the privilege is lost.

Waiver of privilege is possible, as privilege belongs to the client and not to the lawyer. If the client instructs his lawyer to waive privilege, the lawyer must do so.

Documents disclosed by mistake *might* lose their privileged nature. This principle might have been considered by an Irish court in *People (A-G) v Coleman* [1945] I.R. 237, discussed earlier, where the prosecution was allowed to rely on a note written by the accused to his solicitor, which he dropped whilst being visited in prison by his wife. The Court, however, admitted the evidence on another basis, namely that the accused intended to subornate witnesses, and accordingly the privilege was lost on that basis. In a later, English case, *R. v Tompkins* (1977) 67 Cr.App.R. 1, the Court allowed the prosecution to lead into evidence an inculpatory note which had been dropped by defence counsel on the floor in the courtroom and which was retrieved by the prosecution counsel. On appeal, the Court held that although the note was privileged from production, it was admissible once it was in the possession of the prosecution. The *Tompkins* decision followed the earlier decision of the Court of Appeal in England of *Calcraft v Guest* [1898] 1 Q.B. 759 (C.A.) where privileged documents, accidentally left in the possession of witnesses, were illegally copied. These witnesses were allowed to introduce the copies in order to prove their contents. The Court of Appeal held that it would be permissible to admit such evidence even when the documents had fallen into another's hands by unlawful or improper means. This approach has now been rejected by the English courts.

Key Principle: Despite the general rule that once a document has been inspected by other parties it is too late to claim privilege, the court has power to intervene if the inspection has been procured by fraud or if the inspecting party realised, or should have realised, that there had been a mistake.

Guinness Peat Properties v Fitzroy Robinson Partnership [1987]

Guinness Peat Properties ("GPP"), building developers, engaged Fitzroy Robinson Partnership ("FRP"), to act as architects for the construction of an office building. Subsequently, GPP notified FRP of a design fault in part of the building and stated that they intended to hold the defendants responsible for the cost of remedying the defect. FRP forwarded the claim to their insurers, and included with the claim their own views on the merits of the claim and estimated the cost of repairs at £50,000. GPP sued FRP, claiming the cost of repairs and loss of rent. In the course of discovery, the solicitors for FRP inadvertently failed to claim privilege for the letter by FRP containing their views on the merits of GPP's claim, and left the letter in the files of correspondence disclosed to GPP's solicitors and experts, one of whom took a copy of the letter. When FRP's solicitors realised that the letter had been disclosed, they applied for an order restraining GPP from making any use of it at the trial. The judge held that the letter was privileged and that that privilege had not been lost by reason of the fact that the letter had been disclosed and inspected. GPP appealed, arguing that once a privileged document was disclosed and inspected, privilege was irretrievably lost.

Held: The Court of Appeal dismissed the appeal and confirmed that the privilege was not lost. Although the general rule was that once a document had been inspected, it was too late to claim privilege, the court had power, under its equitable jurisdiction, to intervene if the inspection had been procured by fraud or if the inspecting party realised, on inspection, that he had been permitted to see the document only because of an obvious mistake. On the facts, GPP's solicitors must have realised that they had been permitted to see the document because of an obvious mistake by FRP's solicitors and FRP, on realising the mistake, had acted promptly in claiming privilege for the letter. *Guinness Peat Properties Ltd v Fitzroy Robinson Partnership (a firm)* [1987] 2 All E.R. 716; [1987] 1 W.L.R. 1027.

"WITHOUT PREJUDICE"

Communications between solicitors that attempt to settle a dispute are commonly described as "without prejudice" communications. This is because very often the phrase "without prejudice" appears at the top of the solicitor's letter. The reason why privilege attaches to such communications is that this practice encourages settlements. Without the rule, any concession made during a negotiation would be admissible if the case went to court and if this were allowed, fewer negotiations would take place, as parties would not be prepared to make concessions which could later be used against them.

Key Principle: To succeed in a claim of privilege under this heading it is vital that the party claiming the privilege show that the communication was made in a genuine attempt to settle the dispute, and with the intention that if the negotiations proved unsuccessful, the communication could not be disclosed in any proceedings without the consent of the party.

Ryan v Connolly [2001]

Desmond Ryan was knocked off his motorbike by a car driven by Anne Marie Connolly and owned by Michael Connolly. Ryan was injured and the motorbike badly damaged. Ryan's solicitors informed the Connollys that they would be claiming for the injuries and loss and requested that their letter be forwarded to the Connollys' insurers.

All subsequent correspondence between the parties was headed "without prejudice". By letter dated July 11, 1995 the insurer sought certain information from Ryan's solicitor and stated that, on receipt of this letter and having concluded their investigation, they would be in a position to make a decision regarding liability. Ryan's solicitor replied on September 1, 1995, providing the information requested. By letter dated July 9, 1996 the insurer requested Ryan's solicitor to advise if he was in a position to discuss a settlement at that time. The solicitor replied on July 24, 1996 and stated that he was awaiting an up-to-date medical report and would contact the insurer as soon as one was obtained. By letters dated March 13, 1997, October 30, 1997 and January 27, 1998 (which were not replied to by Ryan's solicitor) the insurer requested the solicitor to advise as to whether he was in a position to have settlement discussions. On July 2, 1998— at which point the claim was barred as the statutory limitation period of three years within which proceedings had to be instituted had expired—the insurer wrote a letter requesting Ryan's solicitor to advise if he was in a position to meet for "without prejudice" talks.

On April 30, 1998 Ryan's solicitor requested the insurer to nominate a solicitor to accept service of proceedings. These proceedings were instituted by way of plenary summons dated December 11, 1998 and a statement of claim was delivered on June 11, 1999.

In their defence, delivered on July 14, 1999, the Connollys pleaded that the action was statute-barred pursuant to s.11(2)(b) of the Statute of Limitations 1957, as amended. Ryan argued that the conduct of the insurer on behalf of the Connollys had caused Ryan to refrain from issuing proceedings within the period prescribed by statute, and therefore the Connollys were estopped from relying on the provisions of the Statute of Limitations 1957.

The High Court held that the Connollys were not entitled to rely on the defence that the action was statute-barred, and they appealed this decision to the Supreme Court.

Held: The Supreme Court allowed the appeal and held that the Connollys were entitled to rely on a defence under the Statute of Limitations 1957. The Court confirmed that the policy behind the concept of "without prejudice" was to encourage parties to settle their disputes without resort to litigation. However, the presence of the heading "without prejudice" on a particular document does not automatically make the document privileged. In any case, where the privilege is claimed but challenged, the court is entitled to examine the document in order to determine whether it is of such a nature as to attract privilege. Although the "without prejudice" rule is firmly based on considerations of public policy, it should not be applied in so inflexible a manner as to produce injustice. The court could read the letter and decide whether that letter had caused the other party to refrain from issuing proceedings. The court was entitled to examine the "without prejudice" correspondence for the purpose of determining whether the circumstances were such that the defendants should be precluded from maintaining their plea under the Statute of Limitations.

When the court did examine the letter in question, it found that there was nothing to indicate that the insurer would not be relying on a defence under the Statute of Limitations, and the court therefore held that the Connollys were entitled to mount that defence to the claim. *Desmond Ryan v Michael Connolly and Anne Marie Connolly* [2001] 2 I.L.R.M. 174.

THE RIGHT TO SILENCE

The privilege against self-incrimination is often referred to as the "right to silence". The three main components of this right are the right of an accused not to give evidence at his trial; the right of a suspect to remain silent while being questioned; and the right of witnesses (as distinct from the accused) not to answer any question which would incriminate them.

Key Principle: A suspect has the right to remain silent during questioning.

Heaney and McGuinness v Ireland [1996]

Heaney and McGuinness were detained in terms of the Offences Against the State Act of 1939, on suspicion of being members of the IRA and for being involved in a bombing. They were asked to provide details of their movements and activities in the preceding days. They refused to do so and were charged and convicted under s.52 of the 1939 Act, and sentenced to six months' imprisonment, the maximum penalty allowed in terms of the section.

Section 52 says that:

> "Whenever a person is detained in custody under the provisions in that behalf contained in Part IV of this Act, any member of the Garda Síochána may demand of such person, at any time while he is so detained, a full account of such person's movements and actions during any specified period and all information in his possession in relation to the commission or intended commission by another person of any offence under any section or sub-section of this Act or any scheduled offence.

> If any person, of whom any such account or information as is mentioned in the foregoing sub-section of this section is demanded under that sub-section by a member of the Garda Síochána, fails or refuses to give to such member such account or any such information or gives to such member any account or information which is false or misleading, he shall be guilty of an offence under this section and shall be liable on summary conviction thereof to imprisonment for a term not exceeding six months."

At the time of the hearing Heaney and McGuinness had completed their prison sentences. They nevertheless appealed their convictions. The High Court confirmed the convictions, finding that the right of a suspect not to answer questions was founded on Art.38, rather than Art.40 of the Constitution. The High Court found that the State was entitled to curtail that right.

Heaney and McGuinness appealed this finding to the Supreme Court, arguing that s.52 was unconstitutional, as it breached the right to silence.

Held: The Supreme Court upheld the finding of the High Court that s.52 does not infringe the Constitution, albeit on a different basis to that of the High Court. The Supreme Court held that the right to silence is but a corollary to the freedom of expression that is conferred by Art.40 of the Constitution, and so the right to remain silent can be qualified. An obvious example of the immunity being expressly abrogated is the accused who elects to give evidence (s.1(e) of the Criminal Justice (Evidence) Act, 1924). There is a dichotomy between the absolute entitlement to silence as against the entitlement to remain silent when to answer would give rise to self-incrimination. Where a person is totally innocent of any wrongdoing, there is no reason to insist on his constitutional right to remain silent. The Court therefore approached the matter as an encroachment against the right not to have to say anything that might afford evidence that is self-incriminating.

The Court held that there are many statutes which impinge on the right to silence, demonstrating a clear legislative intent to abrogate, to various extents, the right to silence, in a number of contrasting circumstances. In terms of s.52, the power given to the Garda Síochána by the section was proportionate to the objects to be achieved by the legislation. Accordingly, there was a proper proportionality in the provision between any infringement of the citizen's rights and the entitlement of the State to protect itself. The appeal was refused. *Heaney and McGuinness v Ireland* [1996] 1 I.R. 580.

Commentary
Heaney and McGuinness appealed this decision to the European Court of Human Rights (*Heaney and McGuinness v Ireland* (2001) 33 E.H.R.R. 264). Here, it was held that s.52 breached their right to a fair trial under Art.6 of the Convention. The Court held that by compelling them to provide information relating to charges against them under that Act, this destroyed the very essence of their privilege against self-incrimination and their right to remain silent.

DPP v Finnerty [1999]
Joseph Finnerty was charged with two counts of rape. During the

trial, whilst cross-examining the complainant, the defence counsel suggested to her that the accused would testify that the version of events as she described them did not happen, and that he would offer a contradictory version. Prosecuting counsel sought leave to introduce evidence that Finnerty, during his detention in the Garda station, had not given this version of events; in fact, he had not offered any version, and this would be relevant when the jury came to assess his credibility. The trial judge ruled that the evidence was admissible and Finnerty was cross-examined as to what had happened in the Garda station.

Finnerty's counsel asked the trial judge to discharge the jury on the basis that he had effectively abolished the accused's right to silence by drawing attention to his refusal to answer questions while in custody. The trial judge declined to discharge the jury and Finnerty was convicted.

The Court of Criminal Appeal upheld the decision of the trial judge and turned down Finnerty's appeal. He appealed this finding to the Supreme Court.

Held: The Supreme Court allowed the appeal, quashed the conviction, and ordered a retrial. It held that the right to silence was a constitutional right and any abridgement of that right, such as allowing inferences to be drawn from an accused's silence, must be expressly legislated for and proportionate to the objects to be achieved by that legislation. Although the section in question did abridge the right to silence, this was only in specified circumstances—it did not constitute a general abridgement of the right.

The Supreme Court held further that no cross-examination by the prosecution should be permitted concerning the refusal of an accused to answer questions during the course of his detention, and, in his instructions to the jury, the trial judge should, in general, make no reference to the fact that the accused refused to answer questions during the course of his detention. *The People (at the suit of the Director of Public Prosecutions) v Joseph Finnerty* [1999] 4 I.R. 364.

Key Principle: A court is not obliged to draw adverse inferences from the silence of the accused when being questioned.

Rock v Ireland and The Attorney-General [1997]

Paul Rock was arrested after being found in a cubicle of the public toilet at the Burlington Hotel, Dublin, with counterfeit banknotes to the value of U.S.$200,000. When questioned, Rock refused to answer any questions except to give his name and address. Sections 18 and 19 of the Criminal Justice Act of 1984 permit a court to draw adverse inferences from the failure of the accused to explain the presence of an object, substance or mark. Rock was cautioned about these sections and their effect, but persisted in his refusal to answer questions. He was convicted and appealed his conviction to the High Court on the grounds that ss.18 and 19 infringed his right to silence and the presumption of innocence. The High Court rejected the appeal. Rock appealed this decision to the Supreme Court.

Held: While a court might draw inferences from an accused's failure or refusal to account for the presence of an object, substance or mark in the circumstances provided for in s.18 of the Act of 1984, it was not obliged to draw any inference from such failure or refusal.

Neither the presumption of innocence, nor the burden of proof, which rests on the prosecution in a criminal charge, was in any way affected by these provisions, which merely provided a factor which might be adduced as evidence in the course of the trial. The right to silence was implicit in the Constitution but was not absolute and was subject to public order and morality. If inferences were properly drawn, such inferences amounted only to evidence requiring corroboration; they were not to be taken as proof.

The function of the Court was not to decide whether a perfect balance had been achieved between the accused's right to silence and the constitutional duty imposed on the State to protect citizens from attacks on their person or property, but whether in restricting individual constitutional rights, the legislature had acted within the range of what is permissible.

There were two important limiting factors at work: first, that an inference could not form the basis for a conviction in the absence of other evidence; and, secondly, that an inference adverse to the accused could only be drawn where the court deemed it proper to do so. For example, a court could refuse to allow an inference in circumstances where its prejudicial effect would wholly outweigh its probative value as evidence. The appeal was refused and Rock's conviction was confirmed. *Paul Rock v Ireland and the Attorney-General* [1997] 3 I.R. 384.

Commentary
Adverse inferences can only be drawn if permitted by statute. This was confirmed by the Supreme Court in *People (DPP) v Finnerty* [1999] 4 I.R. 364, discussed earlier.

Several statutes permit adverse inferences to be drawn from an accused's decision to remain silent after he has been arrested. Sections 18 and 19 of the Criminal Justice Act 1984 permit adverse inferences to be drawn from an accused's failure to explain his possession of a particular object (s.18) or his presence at a particular place (s.19) when asked to do so by the Gardaí. Section 3 of the Criminal Justice (Forensic Evidence) Act 1990 permits adverse inferences to be drawn from an accused's refusal to provide samples for DNA testing. Section 7 of the Criminal Justice (Drug Trafficking) Act 1996 and s.5 of the Offences Against the State (Amendment) Act 1998 both provide that adverse inferences can be drawn from an accused's failure to mention any fact while in custody which he later relies on for his defence.

What is important is the point made in the above decision—the statutes *permit* an inference to be made, they do not oblige the court to make an inference. Accordingly, the discretion of the trial judge is intact. If the statute went further than that, it might create an irrebuttable presumption, the like of which was struck down in *Maher v Attorney-General*, discussed in Chapter 1.

Key Principle: A witness has the right to refuse to answer a question on the grounds that to answer the question would incriminate that witness, but this right can be removed by statute.

Re (In the matter of) National Irish Bank (No.1) **[1999]**

Part II of the Companies Act of 1990 provides a mechanism for the investigation of companies by inspectors appointed in terms of the Act. These inspectors are given the power to compel answers and to compel the production of relevant documents from all officers and agents of a company whose affairs are under investigation.

Section 18 of the Companies Act provides:

"An answer given by a person to a question put to him in exercise of powers conferred by -

a. section 10;

b. section 10 as applied by sections 14 and 17; or

c. rules made in respect of the winding-up of companies whether by the Court or voluntarily under section 68 of the Courts of Justice Act, 1936, as extended by section 312 of the Principal Act; may be used in evidence against him, and a statement required by section 224 of the Principal Act may be used in evidence against any person making or concurring in making it."

Two inspectors were appointed by the High Court on the application of the Minister for Enterprise and Employment, in terms of s.8(1) of the Companies Act, to investigate and report on the improper charging of interest, the improper charging of fees and the improper removal of funds from the accounts of customers of National Irish Bank ("NIB") during the period 1988 to 1998.

The inspectors planned to conduct their investigation in two distinct stages. The first stage would be an information-gathering exercise by way of informal interviews. If the findings of the first stage indicated that "adverse conclusions" could be drawn in relation to certain individuals, a second stage would ensue, consisting of a hearing at which such individuals could have legal representation, could cross-examine witnesses, and could give evidence themselves.

The inspectors asked the High Court for directions as to whether persons from whom information, documents or evidence was sought by the inspectors were entitled to refuse to answer questions put by the inspectors or to refuse to provide documents to the inspectors on the grounds that the answers or documents might tend to incriminate them.

Held: The High Court repeated the principles laid down in *Heaney*, namely, that the privilege against self-incrimination was a correlative right to the constitutional guarantee of freedom of expression, and therefore the so-called right to silence was not an absolute right and could be abrogated, expressly or impliedly, by statute. In testing the statute, a proportionality test had to be applied. The Court had to decide whether the restriction placed on the right to silence by the statute was any greater than was necessary to enable the State to fulfil its obligations under the Constitution. The only entitlement expressly given to a person to refuse to answer a question which might tend to incriminate him, was where such an answer would disclose information which was the subject of legal professional privilege. On the facts of this case, s.10 of the Companies Act abrogated the privilege against self-incrimination and, accordingly, a person could not refuse to answer questions on the grounds that such answers might incriminate him. Section 10 was constitutional in that the abrogation of the right to silence contained in the section was no greater than was necessary to enable the State to fulfil its constitutional obligations.

The Supreme Court confirmed the decision of the High Court, adding that answers compelled under s.10 were not admissible in any subsequent criminal trial. *In the matter of National Irish Bank Ltd (under investigation) and in the matter of the Companies Act, 1990 (No 1)* [1999] 3 I.R. 145.

JOURNALISTIC "PRIVILEGE"

Journalists often assert a right not to disclose their sources. Although some call this a privilege, this label is not strictly accurate. In practice, a court will respect the confidentiality of the sources only if there is another way to obtain the information, assuming that the information is relevant to the issues before the court. Where there is no other way of obtaining that relevant information, the court will order the journalist to disclose his sources of information.

Key Principle: A judge might agree to keep confidential the identity of persons supplying information to journalists if the lives of those persons could be endangered were their identities revealed.

Burke v Central Independent Television plc [1994]

William Burke, Francis Cahill, Thomas Cahill, James Drumm, Alfred Hannaway, John O'Neill and Desmond Wilson claimed damages for libel. They claimed that C.I.T. had broadcast a television programme which claimed that they used the premises of their company, Conway Street Community Enterprises Project Ltd. as the financial nerve centre of a terrorist organisation (the IRA); that James Drumm had engaged in criminal activities; and that Thomas

Cahill was one of four people controlling the financial affairs of the IRA.

In preparation for the forthcoming trial, the parties consented to orders of discovery. However, C.I.T. objected to producing certain documents for inspection which would, or would be likely to, lead to the identification of its sources of information on the grounds that the lives of these informants (including an undercover police officer) would be in grave danger, and that the information contained in the documents was supplied on an undertaking of confidentiality. The television company also argued that current affairs programmes provided valuable information to the public, but could not do so if the safety of contributors was put at risk.

The High Court ordered the television company to produce the documents, and upheld an earlier decision (*Re Kevin O'Kelly* (1974) 108 I.L.T.R.) in holding that Irish courts did not accept a privilege from production of documents based solely on a promise of confidentiality, and that journalists did not enjoy any special rights or privileges to protect their informants from disclosure. The High Court did, however, order that the documents did not have to be produced for at least another six weeks, to enable C.I.T. to appeal to the Supreme Court.

Held: The Supreme Court held that its function was to resolve a conflict between two aspects of the public interest—namely, the protection of citizens from the risk of death or bodily injury and the protection and vindication of the good names of the plaintiffs. The right to protection of life and bodily integrity must take precedence over a citizen's right to protection or vindication of his good name. The appeal was upheld and the sources were not revealed. *William Burke, Francis Cahill, Thomas Cahill, Conway Street Community Enterprises Project Ltd, James Drumm, Alfred Hannaway, John O'Neill and Desmond Wilson v Central Independent Television plc* [1994] 2 I.R. 61.

Commentary

It is important to note that the Supreme Court did not recognise that journalists were entitled to refuse to disclose their sources as a matter of "privilege". In fact, the Supreme Court confirmed the earlier case that had rejected the notion of journalistic privilege, namely *Re Kevin O'Kelly* (1974) 108 I.L.T.R. 97. The basis on which the sources were protected was that the life and integrity of the sources was more important than the good names of the plaintiffs.

INFORMER PRIVILEGE

Informer privilege has been recognised by Irish courts on the basis that if their identities were revealed, they would be in danger, and if no privilege existed, there would be fewer informers, which would make crime detection more difficult. Initially, informer privilege only applied to police informers, but the privilege has been extended, with the court having to weigh the public interest in preserving the anonymity of the informer against the public interest in hearing the evidence.

Key Principle: The question of informer privilege does not only apply in criminal law matters, but can apply in civil matters as well.

Director of Consumer Affairs v Sugar Distributors Ltd [1991]

As a result of a complaint made against Sugar Distributors Ltd by another company, ASI International Foods, the Director of Consumer Affairs carried out an investigation and instituted proceedings against Sugar Distributors Ltd for alleged anti-competitive behaviour in breach of the Restrictive Practices Act 1972, and the Restrictive Practices (Groceries) Order 1987. It was alleged that Sugar Distributors Ltd purchased sugar from a potential competitor to keep its monopoly of the Irish sugar market, and entered into an arrangement with the owner of a retail grocers in Boyle, County Roscommon, by which it replaced his stock of the competitor's sugar with its own sugar.

Sugar Distributors Ltd sought discovery of various documents relating to the complaint. The Director of Consumer Affairs claimed privilege in respect of certain correspondence between the complainant company and another party, which was obtained by the Director of Consumer Affairs as part of the complaint made by the complainant company.

Held: The High Court upheld the claim of privilege. The court held that it was in the public interest that the public service was functioning properly and it was also in the public interest in the prevention and detection of crime that informers could remain anonymous.

On the facts, the court held that in order to effectively carry out its statutory law-enforcement functions, the Director of Consumer Affairs needed to be able to assure the public that complaints made of another party's breach of a statutory order would be treated in confidence. The documents would be privileged unless they tended to show that Sugar Distributors Ltd had not committed the wrongful act as alleged. The court would need to examine the documents to see if the claim of privilege was justified. *Director of Consumer Affairs and Fair Trade v Sugar Distributors Ltd* [1991] 1 I.R. 225.

Goodman International v Hamilton (No.3) [1993]

Tomas MacGiolla, Dick Spring and Barry Desmond were members of the Oireachtas. They made serious allegations against Goodman International before Hamilton J., the sole member of a tribunal of inquiry into irregularities in the beef-processing industry. The three TDs thereafter refused to disclose the identities of the persons who had supplied them with the information upon which these allegations were based.

Despite the fact that the TDs did not enjoy parliamentary protection for things said outside the Houses of the Oireachtas or to the Tribunal, Hamilton J. ruled that the TDs were entitled to refuse to disclose to the Tribunal the identities of their informants because the common law recognised informer privilege.

Goodman International applied for a judicial review of Hamilton J.'s ruling, arguing that it was wrong in law.

Held: The High Court held that it was unnecessary to decide whether the relationship between a member of the public and a TD, where the member of the public gave that TD confidential information of public interest, fell within the Wigmore test as laid out in *Cook v Carroll*. The Court held that the issue needed to be decided based on the facts before the Court, which had a direct public interest dimension far beyond the mere private interest in confidentiality. The Court held that the Wigmore rules are appropriate where the privilege is sought in respect of a private relationship analogous to that of lawyer and client, but not where a direct public interest is a major factor in favour of upholding the privilege claimed.

The Court held that, as a general rule, the exclusion of admissible and relevant evidence was contrary to the public interest in the administration of justice. However, the Court had discretion to uphold a refusal to give evidence, provided it was clearly demonstrated that the public interest would be better served by excluding such evidence.

On the facts, it was important that the informants reasonably expected their identities to remain secret, and the fact that Hamilton J. had stated that hearsay evidence would not be admitted to undermine the good names of Laurence Goodman or Goodman International, the non-disclosure of the identities of the informants was justified. The application for review was refused. *Goodman International and Laurence Goodman v The Honourable Mr Justice Liam Hamilton, sole member of the Tribunal of Inquiry into the Beef Processing Industry, The Attorney-General, Pat Rabbitte, Tomas MacGiolla, Dick Spring and Barry Desmond (No. 3)* [1993] 3 I.R. 320.

MARITAL PRIVILEGE

Marital privilege is the privilege enjoyed by a husband and wife not to disclose any communications made by either spouse during their marriage. Either spouse can choose to waive this privilege (without the consent of the other spouse), which means that a spouse is competent but not compellable to testify against the other spouse. The Criminal Evidence Act 1992 makes the spouse of an accused competent to testify on behalf of the prosecution and compellable in certain limited circumstances. However, s.26 of the 1992 Act states: "nothing in this Act shall affect the right of a spouse to marital privacy".

Key Principle: Marital privilege does not originate in the common law, but is statutory in origin. In Ireland, it also has constitutional support in the form of the right to marital privacy.

McGhee v Attorney-General [1974]

Mary McGhee and her husband had four children, who were all born between December 1968 and November 1970, a period of only 23 months, the youngest children being twins. After the birth of her second child, she had been advised by her doctor that a further pregnancy would be extremely unwise because of the risk of recurrence of a cerebral thrombosis which, if not fatal, would be likely to result in paralysis. She was unable to operate properly the temperature method of birth control and, because of her history of thrombosis, oral contraceptives were unsuitable for her. On medical advice, she was fitted with a diaphragm. During a subsequent check-up, it was discovered that she was again pregnant with the twins, only three months after the birth of her second child. With each of her three pregnancies Mrs McGhee had very serious complications, including toxaemia, a urinary tract infection, high blood-pressure, and a cerebral thrombosis or stroke, and she was lucky to have survived. During her third pregnancy she also developed an infection and toxaemia, and was very ill. She gave birth to twins, which were premature, on November 15, 1970. She had very serious complications during, and subsequent to, the birth of the twins.

Given this history, Mr and Mrs McGhee decided that they should have no more children. Mrs McGhee was fitted with another diaphragm by her doctor and was advised to use a spermicidal jelly with the diaphragm. The doctor prescribed "Staycept Jelly", but as it was not manufactured in Ireland, arrangements were made to import the jelly from England.

As this jelly was a "contraceptive" and therefore prohibited within the meaning of s.17(4) of the Criminal Law Amendment Act of 1935, it was seized by Customs.

Mrs McGhee argued that s.17(4) was unconstitutional as it failed to recognise the right of her and her husband to make a private decision about their family and her life within the home and that by frustrating this decision it endangered her life within her home.

Held: The Supreme Court, by a majority of four to one (Fitzgerald C.J. dissenting) agreed that s.17(4) was unconstitutional as being an unjustified invasion into marital privacy. The majority of the Court held that it is a matter exclusively for the husband and wife to decide how many children they wish to have and it would be quite outside the competence of the State to dictate or prescribe the number of children they should have. This also meant that a husband and wife had a correlative right to agree to have no children. The sexual life of a husband and wife is of necessity, and by its nature, an area of particular privacy. If the husband and wife decide to limit their family or to avoid having children by use of contraceptives, it is a matter peculiarly within the joint decision of the husband and wife, and one into which the State cannot intrude unless its intrusion is justified by the exigencies of the common good, which was not the case here. Article 41 of the Constitution guarantees the husband and wife protection against any such invasion of their privacy by the State. It follows that the use of contraceptives by them within that marital privacy is equally guaranteed against such invasion and, as such, assumes the status of a right so guaranteed by the Constitution. If this right cannot be directly invaded by the State, it follows that it cannot be frustrated by the State taking measures to ensure that the exercise of that right is rendered impossible. Section 17 of the Act of 1935, insofar as it unreasonably restricted the availability of contraceptives for use within marriage, was inconsistent with the provisions of Art.41 of the Constitution for being an unjustified invasion of the privacy of husband and wife and their sexual relations with one another. *Mary McGhee v the Attorney-General and the Revenue Commissioners* [1974] I.R. 284.

Commentary

The right to claim privilege usually means that, whilst under oath, the witness can refuse to answer certain questions or produce certain evidence. In other words, privilege is usually distinguished from the issue of the overall competence and compellability of a witness. In England, it has been held in *R. v Ian Pitt* [1983] Q.B. 25, that marital privilege is different in that once a spouse elects to take the witness stand and the oath where the other spouse is the accused, the privilege is lost completely. In other words, the privilege is such that the person claiming it can refuse to take the oath or the stand, but once a spouse elects to give evidence, they can be asked any question that could be asked of an ordinary witness, and cannot thereafter refuse to answer any specific question on the grounds of marital privilege.

The *McGhee* decision confirms that marital privacy is protected in Ireland by the Constitution (unlike England) and s.26 of the Criminal Evidence Act recognises the concept of marital privacy (whilst simultaneously eroding it). In Ireland it might be argued that if a spouse testifies in a trial of the other spouse, but her testimony is limited to a specific factual incident and no mention is ever made of any conversation or communication with her accused husband, she should be entitled to invoke martial privilege if asked a question during her cross-examination about any conversation or communication between her and her husband. This question has not been explored by our courts and remains moot.

SACERDOTAL PRIVILEGE

Sacerdotal privilege is the privilege relating to communications between priest and parishioner.

Key Principle: Sacerdotal privilege means that a priest is entitled to refuse to disclose communications between himself and a parishioner. It is, accordingly, a unique form of privilege, as generally privilege belongs to the person imparting the confidential information, as opposed to the one receiving it.

Cook v Carroll [1945]

Thomas Carroll was told by the daughter of Annie Cook that he had made her pregnant. Carroll went straight to his parish priest, the Rev. W.J. Behan. The priest sent his car to fetch the girl. He then counselled the parties, in an attempt to avert a public scandal. Fr Behan was unsuccessful, and Mrs Cook sued Carroll for the seduction of her daughter.

As the meeting was a "without prejudice" meeting, anything said at the meeting would normally have been inadmissible. However, at the trial, both Carroll and the girl testified about what was said at the meeting, although their respective recollections were contradictory. Mrs Cook called the priest as a witness, in order to corroborate an allegation of some admission made by Carroll. Fr Behan refused to testify and he was fined for contempt of court. Fr Behan did not challenge this finding, but the seduction action went on appeal to the High Court, and the Court had an opportunity to consider the issue of sacerdotal privilege.

Held: The High Court held that the refusal of the priest to give evidence was justified and did not amount to contempt of court. Communications made in confidence to a parish priest in a private consultation between that priest and a parishioner, are privileged. This privilege belongs to the priest, and cannot be waived by the parishioner without the consent of the priest. *Annie Cook v Thomas Carroll* [1945] I.R. 515.

Commentary

A noteworthy aspect of this case is that the court used the principles laid down by the great American jurist, Wigmore, as determining privilege. Wigmore held that for a communication to be privileged four conditions must be satisfied:

1. The communications must originate in the confidence that they will not be disclosed;

2. This element of confidentiality must be essential to the full and satisfactory maintenance of the relation;
3. The relation must be one which, in the opinion of the community, ought to be sedulously fostered; and
4. The injury which would enure to the relation by the disclosure of the communications must be greater than the benefit thereby gained for the correct disposal of litigation.

Here, the court held that the four conditions were satisfied and therefore the communication was privileged. The judge rejected the English law on the matter, as this law had been created after the Reformation, which the Roman Catholic Church regarded as heresy.

The Court held that the privilege belonged to the priest and not to the parishioner, unlike legal privilege, which belongs not to the lawyer, but to the client.

Gavan Duffy J. justified the distinction thus:

"As between himself and his attorney, the client is master of the situation, so that, if he thinks fit to waive his privilege, the privilege disappears and the lawyer, his paid servant, cannot set it up. But the priest is not hired, and a parishioner's waiver of privilege should not, as a matter of course, destroy the priest's right to keep his secret, where the sacerdotal privilege is regulated by law; I am speaking here of confidences outside the confessional, for, as Catholics know, the inviolable secrecy of the sacrament of penance stands alone and unique."

This latter finding, that the privilege belonged to the priest, was clearly an *obiter*, and the judge himself described it as a "corollary" and "not a conclusion of law, but as a strong impression".

Johnston v Church of Scientology [2001]

Johnston sued the Church of Scientology for damages for conspiracy, misrepresentation, breach of constitutional rights, libel, and for the return of monies paid by her to the Church. An order for discovery in general terms was made against the Church, who claimed sacerdotal privilege in respect of certain "counselling notes". Those notes arose from spiritual practices of the Church, known as "auditing" and "training", which were conducted on a one-to-one basis.

Held: The High Court held that the sacerdotal privilege that was the basis of the judgment in *Cook v Carroll* had its origins in pre-Reformation common law antiquity, and it applied only to confessional communications between priest and parishioner. Even if the Court were to accept that Scientology was a religion (which it did not), the absolute unwaivable privilege found in Irish common law to the priest–penitent relationship in the confessional was unique (*sui generis*) and could not be extended to other areas. On the other hand, certain confidential relationships might be protected by privilege, such as counselling, but here the privilege belonged to the client, and could always be waived by the client.

In this case, Johnston was the "client", and therefore could waive privilege, if such were to exist. The documents had to be produced. *Johnston v Church of Scientology Mission of Dublin Ltd* [2001] 1 I.R. 682.

Commentary
This matter went to the Supreme Court on appeal (*Johnston v Church of Scientology Mission of Dublin Ltd* [2001] 1 I.R. 682) but the dispute before that Court was whether the Church of Scientology in Ireland could be ordered to produce documents that were kept in England. The issue of sacerdotal privilege was not explored any further.

Index